Also by Taylor Hartman

THE COLOR CODE

COLOR YOUR FUTURE

*Using the Color Code
to Strengthen Your Character*

Dr. Taylor Hartman

SCRIBNER

SCRIBNER
1230 Avenue of the Americas
New York, NY 10020

SCRIBNER and design are trademarks of Jossey-Bass, Inc.,
used under license by Simon & Schuster, the publisher of this work.

DESIGNED BY ERICH HOBBING

Set in Sabon

Manufactured in the United States of America

1   3   5   7   9   10   8   6   4   2

Library of Congress Cataloging-in-Publication Data is available.

ISBN 0-684-84377-3

A previous edition of this book was published in 1991 as *The Character Code*.

Heartfelt appreciation to:

My wife, Jean, who always believes in me.
My children, Terra, Summer, Mikelle, BreAnne, T.J., who always love me.

Sincere dedication to:

My charactered trainers and patients, who always pay the price,
take the charactered path, and fly with me.

Thanks to:

My editor, Jake Morrissey,
who brought renewed vision and breadth to this work

Contents

PREFACE   9

INTRODUCTION   11

FOREWORD   21

CHAPTER ONE: Four Paths for Life   27

CHAPTER TWO: The Hartman Character Profile   37

CHAPTER THREE: Butterflies   55

CHAPTER FOUR: Step One: Value Yourself   61

CHAPTER FIVE: Step Two: Seek Universal Truth   81

CHAPTER SIX: Step Three: Clean Your Motives   107

CHAPTER SEVEN: Step Four: Focus Your Commitments   127

CHAPTER EIGHT: Step Five: Discover Balance   139

CHAPTER NINE: Step Six: Serve Others   153

Preface

The most important task you will ever take on in your life is to become *charactered.* It is not a single event but rather a journey. It comes more easily to some than it does to others but it nevertheless demands that all who attempt it truly embrace the process.

It's like being physically fit when you're fifty years old. A fifty-year-old must make healthy choices and work diligently to stay in shape; good health doesn't just happen. Becoming charactered also requires a consistent effort to choose healthy attitudes and personality traits that might feel foreign to us but will help us improve our character's health.

You can choose to walk the charactered path at any time in your life. However, becoming charactered requires that you learn basic skills before you can approach more complex ones. It's like learning to read: You master the small words before tackling the longer ones. Then you can begin to put words together and create sentences that are more intricate and meaningful. Developing character is a similar process. As with books, when your reading improves you often discover more complicated, more rewarding books to read, character building offers an increased awareness of life's possibilities. With reading, the greater mastery you have of language, the greater the chance you'll have of experiencing all the book has to offer. With character, the greater mastery you have of the gifts each personality type offers, the greater the possibility of attaining your full potential.

Never underestimate the power of the process of becoming charactered. It is not in the "arriving" that character can best be measured but by the quality of the journey. It's like being in a foreign country with your senses open to the excitement of the adventure. You take nothing for granted but remain constantly alert to learning from the unfamiliar.

Like the caterpillar that was always born to become a butterfly, you were born to become charactered. I hope this book prompts you to start, or continue, your journey.

Introduction

Perhaps, in the final analysis, life is simply about coming home. Webster defines home as a place of origin; a place where one lives. It describes home as "deeply to the center of something" and "feeling an easy competence and familiarity." My book *The Color Code* is a personal guide to bringing you safely home to *you.* If you want to know who you were born to be and what drives you at the very core of your personality, *The Color Code* is a must for you to read and reread as you explore the various relationships of your life.

Once you are clear about who you were innately born to be, the next question one instinctively asks is, "Who was I born to become?" For most people, simply staying with your innate personality is not enough. We want to stretch and learn and leave planet Earth with more life experiences and understanding than when we arrived. We are painfully aware of our natural shortcomings and we seek opportunities to embrace gifts that our fellow sojourners seem to so effortlessly enjoy and express. It is our future character that *Color Your Future* addresses. It focuses on the specific steps we must take in acquiring others' natural gifts of personality that *Color Your Future* is all about.

Once an individual is clear about himself, he must move beyond his natural boundaries to strive for greater self-understanding and true purpose. Learning new methods for experiencing a quality life (i.e., patience, embracing the moment, vision, and compassion) requires tremendous effort as well as humility and courage. Successfully embracing *Color Your Future* depends entirely on how willing you are to venture from the safety of your "innate personality." This is not an

11

adventure for the faint of heart. One must be committed to freeing himself of comfortable limitations in order to create room for foreign gifts known as others' personality strengths. You must be clear about who you innately are and comfortable with yourself before you can effectively embrace new dimensions.

Before embarking on this adventure, a brief refresher about us would be helpful. Let's look inside ourselves and confirm that all is as it should be within before we strike out for new horizons.

CATERPILLARS AND BUTTERFLIES

If you selected symbols for your personality and character, the caterpillar would be your personality, the butterfly your character. Your personality is that innate core of thoughts and feelings that came with you at birth. It is complete at conception. It is present along with various genetically inherited traits, like hair color and blood type, although personality is not genetically linked. That is, it is not inherited from one's parents. Nor does your environment create your core personality. It simply is.

Your personality watches over you and guards you. It makes you different from everyone else and remains rigid and quite resistant to change. It does not easily venture out to experience or understand other personalities until it is comfortable and secure with itself. Like siblings who fight among themselves, you can fight with your own personality, but let outsiders do or say something threatening and watch out! Your personality responds like a mother bear watching over her baby cub. Like the mother bear who allows her cub to fight his own battles when he is grown we, too, react less defensively when we are more comfortable and secure within ourselves.

Despite variations and exceptions, each of us can best identify with only one of the core personality motives. Identifying our core motive places us on the path toward charactered living. Once we discover our core personality, we can accentuate its strengths and overcome its limitations.

Accurately recognizing our strengths and limitations humbles us and invites us to courageously stretch to embrace the innate gifts other personalities bring with them to complete us. Accepting ourselves as caterpillars is essential to appreciating our eventual flight. We must know where we started our personal journey in order to value how far we have come.

My book *The Color Code* provides a personality profile and numerous examples and ideas to help you identify your innate personality. To accurately understand your personality and how you interact with others, read *The Color Code*. However, this introduction also includes a brief outline of each color's innate wants, needs, and motives.

Motives, Needs, Wants for Each Personality

	RED	BLUE	WHITE	YELLOW
MOTIVE	Power	Intimacy	Peace	Fun
NEEDS	To look good (academically)	To be good (morally)	To feel good (inside)	To look good (socially)
	To be right	To be understood	To move at one's own pace	To be liked
	To be respected	To be appreciated	To be respected	To be noticed
	Approval	Acceptance	Acceptance	Approval
WANTS	To hide insecurities (tightly)	To reveal insecurities	To hide insecurities	To hide insecurities (loosely)
	To please self	To please others	To please self/ others	To please others/self
	Leadership	Autonomy	Independence	Freedom
	Challenging adventure	Security	Contentment	Playful adventure

REDS

Reds seek power

Simply stated, Reds want their way. If they have been reared in environments where they were able to manipulate their parents and siblings, they become difficult to manage as they get older. When they have gotten their way for too long, Reds find it very difficult to relinquish their power and freedom to authorities they meet in society (teachers, bosses, police, clergy, military officers).

Reds want to be productive

Reds enjoy productivity, whether it is in school, in their careers, or in their personal relationships. Give them a reason to produce and get out of their way. Reds like to get the job done. They are often workaholics. They will, however, resist being forced to do anything that doesn't interest them.

Reds want to look good to others

Reds need to appear knowledgeable. They crave approval from others for their intelligence and insight. They prefer being respected to being loved. They want to be admired for their logical, practical minds. When you deal with Reds, be precise and factual. Reds are unmoved by tears and/or other needless displays of "weakness."

Reds enjoy a good debate

Reds usually state the facts as they see them, despite their accuracy. They seldom say "in my opinion" before stating their opinions. Too often, Blues, Whites, and Yellows become too emotionally charged over issues with a Red, who is simply enjoying the process of a good debate. While they do enjoy a good power play, Reds shouldn't be taken too seriously all the time.

Reds seek leadership opportunities

Despite the rigidity of law and the military, Reds often seek structures where they can eventually experience leadership. They like to be in the driver's seat. What better "driver's seat" than a judge, a politician, or a general? Red children are often frustrated in school because teachers (often Blue personalities) won't give them opportunities to be in charge. If a Red can get the upper hand, he/she will. Reds are willing to pay a high price in order to lead.

BLUES

Blues are motivated by altruism

Blues love to help others. They seek opportunities to serve others, despite personal sacrifice. Many Blues are uncomfortable doing things solely for themselves. They thrive on social graces and having manners like holding doors open for people, standing up when greeting visitors, and acting appropriately in public places.

Blues enjoy intimacy

More than anything else, Blues want to be loved. A healthy Blue will sacrifice a successful career in order to improve an important relationship. Once considered a female characteristic, this gift of nurturing is more accurately understood as a Blue personality trait.

Blues are gratified when they are listened to, when they feel understood and appreciated. They are notorious for revealing their inadequacies because they value being known and understood by others rather than merely existing in arrogant seclusion. In the eyes of a Blue, being vulnerable is small price to pay for intimacy. Blues suffer more broken hearts than most people, but they also spend more time in love.

Blues need to be appreciated

With Blues, a simple pat on the back will not suffice. Blues expend tremendous effort in "fixing others" and making the world "right." In return, they value knowing that their efforts are appreciated. They need to be thanked and specifically remembered for their good deeds.

They value sincere gratitude. They delight in being remembered on birthdays and other special days, especially if the remembrance is personal, such as a homemade anniversary card, a welcome home party, or any gift with a personal touch. Blues place a high priority on meaningful personal relationships.

Blues are directed by a strong moral conscience

Blues are innately motivated by integrity. They have a moral code that guides them in their decision making, their value judgments, and even their leisure time. Blues enjoy being "good." Of all the personalities as a group, Blues come innately equipped with the strongest moral principles. A Blue would rather lose than cheat. They value trustworthiness.

WHITES

Whites are motivated by peace

Whites will do almost anything to avoid confrontation. They enjoy flowing through life without hassle or needless irritation. "Feeling" good is innately more important to them than "being" good.

Whites need kindness

While Whites respond well to thoughtfulness and amiability, they have a strong, silent stubbornness that surfaces when they are treated unkindly. They resent being scolded and dislike harsh words. They open up to people who are kind and logical but recoil from those who sport hostility. They are tolerant of others and patient with their shortcomings.

Whites enjoy clarity and a low profile

Whites see experiences in life with tremendous clarity. They observe life's twists and human interactions with powerfully accurate perceptions. Whites also enjoy their quiet independence. Whites say very little and others often misinterpret their passivity as ignorance or weakness. Nothing could be further from the truth. Whites are neither ignorant nor weak. They simply prefer to be asked for their opinion before volunteering it. Almost arrogantly, they withhold their insights until they deem the individual worthy of hearing what they have to say. They value the respect of others, but they rarely go out of their way to seek it. They need to be coaxed to talk about their skills, hobbies, and interests.

Whites are independent

Unlike Reds and Blues, who want to control others, Whites seek only to avoid being controlled. They simply refuse to be inappropriately dominated. Whites want to do things their own way, in their own time. They don't ask much of others and resent it when others demand things from them. However, they often comply with unreasonable demands in order to keep the peace and become passive-aggressive by refusing to cooperate at a later time on a completely different issue. However, some Whites simply nod their head in agreement and go off and do exactly what *they* had already planned. They express their anger and frustration only after they can no longer stand being bossed around. Whites don't like to be pushed, and they can be fearsome when they finally "blow up."

Whites are agreeable

Whites are open to the recommendations of others on ways to resolve any and all situations. White executives value new management ideas from employees. White children welcome others' resolutions to their problems. They make agreeable dating partners. They are pleasant to be with and are generally willing to do whatever the other person wants to keep peace. However, Whites want suggestions, not demands.

YELLOWS

Yellows value play

Yellows consider life to be a party, and they are hosting. Motivated to have fun, Yellows can abandon anything when a better offer comes up. They live by the "better offer" theory. In other words, "If it's better, it should be done—and I should be doing it!"

Yellows welcome praise

Yellows need to be noticed. Nothing improves a relationship with a Yellow more than genuine adoration. Yellows need approval and seek to be valued. Yellows often act as though they have the world by the tail. They have their fears and frustrations, which they rarely confide until they know it is safe to do so.

Yellows need intimacy

Yellows often appear so nonchalant that people think they don't care about anything. Not true. Yellows need a great deal of attention. Like the Blues, they are deeply rooted in emotion and like to be stroked. Yellows enjoy touching. To them, physical contact is a direct, comfortable connection.

Yellows want to be popular

Yellows like to be center stage. Looking good socially is very important to them. Friendships command a high priority in their lives because social interaction answers their basic need for approval. Yellows are highly verbal and relish good conversations. They are equally comfortable engaging in a heated debate or chit-chatting at a cocktail party.

Yellows crave action

Easily bored, Yellows seek playful adventure. They cannot sit still for long. They choose friends who, like them, refuse to allow the "boring details" to get in the way of their primary reason for living—to play.

Foreword

Observing a caterpillar's transformation to becoming a butterfly is magical. The process brings with it the same dynamics we experience in our transformation from mere personality to fully charactered souls. It's a lifelong process of becoming fully human, fully alive. Not all caterpillars become butterflies, of course. Some die prematurely by neglecting to take the necessary precautions to enable their survival until the proper time for their "right of passage." Others simply remain on the ground, refusing to risk the unknown challenges of flight.

Caterpillars are not alone. People struggle to experience their true potential in becoming fully charactered human beings as well. Can we lift ourselves from this muddled existence? we wonder.

"Fly!" our inner core whispers. "Fly to greater heights. Experience all you were born to become." *Repeatedly, from deep within us, our better self challenges us to risk the unknown—to break free of our old inadequate patterns and charter a new course for places yet unknown.* "Recreate yourself. Discover your passions. Complete your purpose in life," we hear. At every turn in life we face ourselves. Caterpillars that learn to fly listen to their instincts, their inner voice of truth. Each individual must decide to accept or reject his or her personal flight. Some prefer to continue crawling, like the caterpillar, in established patterns of despondent comfort zones. Some find pleasure enough in merely observing others in flight, satisfied to experience life through the eyes of another. Some fly for a brief time, but ill prepared, they fall victim to unrealistic expectations and ignored danger in their unfamiliar and, perhaps, somewhat "heady" role of being a butterfly.

Still others embrace the challenge to fly and humbly experience new and rewarding horizons throughout their lives.

Wherever you are on your journey in life, I sincerely hope *Color Your Future* will help you embrace yourself, listen to your inner core, and fly.

Our journey together began with my first book, entitled *The Color Code: A New Way to See Yourself, Your Relationships, and Life.* It might just as easily have been entitled *Sudden Identity* because of its revolutionary accuracy in identifying innate personalities and core motivations. Our innate personalities give us personal definition and style. Each personality is driven by an innate core motive and uniquely expresses itself through predictable thought and behavior patterns.

Despite its obvious virtues, personality, like the caterpillar, remains limited. In order to experience the full measure of our creation, we must learn other gifts that are unnatural to us but innately comfortable to other personalities. Each personality (which I define by using color labels), brings unique gifts to share with the other personalities. Reds bring power, vision, focused commitment, leadership, and logic. Blues provide us with intimacy, service, compassion, loyalty, and emotional intuition. Whites entreat us with peace, kindness, balance, acceptance, and clarity. Yellows offer fun, forgiveness, optimism, social celebration, and valuing oneself. Humbly embracing any of these unnatural gifts activates the metamorphosis wherein our personal transformation from caterpillar to butterfly begins to take place.

Flight occurs when we have mastered enough gifts from each of the various personalities to be trusted by our fellow men. Earning this trust requires that we: 1) accurately identify and accept our core personality (color); 2) freely give our innate gifts; and 3) learn, master, and share unnatural (learned) gifts that the other colors bring to our lives. *The Color Code* addresses the process of gaining an accurate understanding of our identity, in other words, who we are. *Color Your Future* addresses the process of embracing all we are capable of becoming.

Flight, as symbolically expressed by the butterfly, is becoming charactered and living a quality life. Flight is not an ultimate end but rather a quality way of seeing life through more rewarding eyes.

The butterfly does not disdain the caterpillar for its limited movement, but rather, respectfully acknowledges it for housing the butterfly through its earlier life journey. Charactered people do not regard limited people as inferior. They appreciate them for their innate gifts of personality and acknowledge their potential. ***Becoming charactered requires the vision to create an ideal picture different from our current picture of reality.*** Without the conflict our vision creates, we would never stretch to bring our ideal picture into focus. To challenge our innate limitations and experience discomfort forces the caterpillar in us to seek the ultimate gift of charactered flight. With time, we will appreciate our years of crawling through life's somewhat desperate moments. Having once been grounded, the butterfly in us appreciates more deeply our developed gift of wings.

Color Your Future is a book for those who yearn to become more; those who want to fly. Unlike the gift of personality you received at birth, the gift of character must be *earned* throughout your lifetime. Becoming charactered is not a onetime opportunity, but a continuous journey, encompassing all the joys and tragedies of being human.

This journey is not for the casual observer or self-appointed critic. *Color Your Future* is for the humble caterpillar that senses his appointed date with destiny and rather than shrink from his appointed "right of passage," embraces his uniquely personal moment in time. This book challenges you to accept your responsibility to become charactered and take flight.

DISCOVER YOUR OPTIMUM MOTIVE

The Color Code defines each color through core personality motives. Reds are driven by power, while Blues are motivated by intimacy. Whites seek peace, while Yellows clearly want to have fun. *Color Your Future **defines character as a learned process driven by the optimum motive of service.*** The more charactered we become, the higher degree of trust we earn, and the greater amount of service we are able to render. Becoming charactered requires a much more rigorous and principled process than merely having a personality, but offers a more powerful reward in the quality of one's life as well. It answers to a higher law than the basic motives of personality.

Unlike the unique personality motives, optimum character motives drive all personalities equally. For example, in order to serve others as dictated by our optimum motive, Yellow personalities, who innately prefer to play, must learn to focus their commitments. Reds are required to be less critical and more patient. Optimum motive demands acceptance and having realistic expectations of the Blues, while Whites are asked to confront their fears of interpersonal conflict and assert themselves. The optimum motive of service becomes our driving core in becoming charactered.

ENJOY SUCCESSFUL RELATIONSHIPS

Color Your Future is easy to read but requires a lifetime to completely understand. One does not become fully charactered without experiencing each step and embracing each of the other colors' gifts. This process requires humility and commitment. Just when I think I understand a particular gift or step, life walks me through it one more time with different players; perhaps a different child, a new employee, or an aging friend. Sometimes the challenge must be faced against a new backdrop in life—perhaps a career change, a financial reversal, or a family crisis.

Each time we choose to walk the higher path and embrace the lessons it has to teach, we become more charactered. Limited personalities reject the invitation. Once we master each of these steps and humbly embrace the gifts each personality brings, we will have earned trust and know the rare, rewarding joy of charactered flight.

What people around the world want most in life is to enjoy successful relationships. *The Color Code* explains why this rarest of treasures is so difficult to accomplish. *Color Your Future* explains how you can make it yours. Specific steps and positive activities are offered throughout this book. Numerous case studies of ordinary people as well as candid revelations about famous celebrities will inspire you to embrace the charactered life. You will discover new possibilities for enhancing your relationships as you consider each step.

Enjoy the miracle of who you were born to become and the magic of taking charactered flight. Once you understand *Color Your Future*, you can never see yourself or others the same again.

COLOR
YOUR FUTURE

✦

CHAPTER ONE

Four Paths for Life

What you are is God's gift to you;
what you become is your gift to God.

There are four clearly defined paths you can choose to walk in life. Your choices include (from most worthwhile to most detrimental): 1) *charactered,* 2) *healthy,* 3) *unhealthy,* 4) *pathological.*

Here's how they are broken down:

Charactered	Healthy	Unhealthy	Pathological
positive traits	positive traits	negative traits	negative traits
of colors from	of color from	of color from	of colors from
outside innate	inside innate	inside innate	outside innate
core personality	core personality	core personality	core personality

THE CHARACTERED PATH

Only quality individuals choose the charactered path. The other three paths will offer a more limited version of life. Charactered people accurately identify and develop the strengths of their core personalities. Furthermore, they stretch to embrace the strengths of other personalities in order to compensate for their innate limitations. Embracing the gifts (strengths) of other colors, charactered people evolve. The more gifts they adopt, the more charactered they become, and the higher they soar in flight.

THE HEALTHY PATH

Healthy individuals are like a caterpillar in its cocoon, almost ready to take flight. Healthy individuals primarily engage life through their strengths. They provide wonderful role models for quality living as seen through the eyes of their particular personality. However, they remain primarily confined to expressing themselves through the strengths of their core color, limiting themselves only to those gifts championed by their particular personality. Expecting them to express the gifts in terms of other colors is often disappointing.

THE UNHEALTHY PATH

Unhealthy individuals begrudgingly remain caterpillars. Strapped by their innate "baggage," they spend their lives confined to and defined by their personality's limitations. Unlike pathological people, however, they remain true to the limitations within their core personality, expressing themselves consistently with their weaknesses. They usually become manipulative in order to justify and rationalize their limited (and often pathetic) lives.

THE PATHOLOGICAL PATH

Pathological individuals are severely handicapped human beings. In the context of this book, they would most likely even deny their existence as caterpillars. "Don't label me!" they demand. "I'm *all* the colors, depending on the circumstances. I'm a rainbow!" *Pathological people are completely out of touch with who they were innately born to be, and haven't a clue as to what they are capable of becoming.*

They express themselves throughout life in the limitations of all colors except their own. They are inconsistent and untrustworthy. While some are extremely intelligent, their lack of congruence creates a lack of clarity in their thought and behavior in all colors except their own. If you could see into the heart of these individuals, you would find serious confusion, powerlessness, and insecurity. They are often incapable of using their natural strengths and yet, ironically, refuse to live within their core personality limitations either.

CHOOSE YOUR PATH

Everybody must choose his/her destiny. The level of health you aspire to will ultimately determine the quality of your life. While there are great latitudes within each level, from charactered to pathological, each level has certain requirements: less healthy individuals typically place greater emphasis on themselves, and most often at the expense of others.

For example, all individuals who walk the charactered path learn and embrace gifts other personalities bring at birth. The more charactered people become, the less concerned they are with themselves. Their focus blends self-love with concern for the quality of others' lives. The people who walk the healthy path discover their core motives and bless others with the strengths from their color. Unhealthy people share a common bond by choosing to see life primarily through their innate dysfunctional limitations. Less healthy individuals typically place greater emphasis on themselves, and most often at the expense of others. Individuals seeking the pathological path commonly present themselves as angry, self-obsessed, and spiritually dysfunctional.

Why Choose the Charactered Path?

Character is defined as "learned" gifts. The optimum motive for becoming charactered is service. Becoming trustworthy to serve requires us to be accountable for our innate strengths, limitations, and motives. To earn trust requires humility, courage, grace, and mastering the six steps of character.

The optimum motive of service drives us to stretch beyond our raw beginnings. While personalities are limited, character is not. Seeking to bless the lives of others challenges us to stretch in order to develop gifts where our innate personalities are limited. Character will not always equate with financial prosperity, but it will *always* enhance the quality of our lives.

Becoming charactered is an evolutionary process that will not appear the same to each color. Since character is "learned," what is character to a Red may look different to a Blue, White, or Yellow. Each color comes with inherent gifts that, when embraced by the other colors, become character. However, these same gifts remain defined as personality to the individual who brings them from birth.

The following case histories may help you identify your current path and level of functioning. I hope *Color Your Future* will help you choose the charactered path.

Which Path Have You Chosen to Walk?

> *Two roads diverged in a wood and I,*
> *I took the road less traveled . . .*
> —ROBERT FROST

THE CHARACTERED PATH

Charactered people will always be best remembered for the unnatural gifts they stretch to develop and freely share with others throughout life.

Lecturing on *The Color Code,* I was intrigued one night when a gentleman, highly regarded for his expertise in early American history, approached me following my lecture and corrected a perception of mine. I had stated that Patrick Henry, one of America's Founding Fathers, had a Blue personality. He cited numerous references validating his position that Patrick Henry was clearly a Red personality rather than a Blue. Thanking him for his insights, I left rather puzzled.

Highly respected as a businessman with a brilliant political future, many felt certain that Patrick Henry was destined to be the president of the United States, when tragically, his wife became despondent and mentally ill. While Americans remain rather unforgiving of this illness, Patrick Henry's peers were brutal, believing that mental illness was a disease linked with religious impropriety, and often condemning mentally ill patients to a life void of human decency. Their society generally believed that diminished mental capacity indicated satanic

30

possession and shunned the victim, often placing them behind bars to die in total isolation on slabs of cold cement.

To a Red Patrick Henry, mental illness did not make sense. He didn't understand or believe in it, but he recognized that his wife, by some bizarre twist of fate, was suffering tremendous pressure from the society they had once successfully embraced together.

Politically astute, Patrick Henry carefully deliberated over his dilemma. Should he dispose of his beloved wife and pursue the prestigious career he rightly deserved, or should he forsake his opportunities to care for the woman he loved? His character intact, his decision made, Patrick Henry returned home and closed the curtains at their home, and consequently the curtains on his promising career. He cared for his wife for months with compassion and genuine loyalty until the day she died with him at her side.

So compassionate and self-sacrificing (innate Blue gifts) were his acts of love that seeing him as a Red puzzled me. But suddenly I understood. I remembered a police officer who had attended one of my earliest seminars, and we could not determine his core color. Was he a Red or a Blue? His heart said Red. His actions said Blue. As we journeyed back through his life, we discovered the answer. His wife had fallen ill, and for many years, he nursed her and stood faithfully by her. Adopting these Blue gifts necessarily caused him to eventually think and behave like a Blue. While maintaining his core Red identity, he successfully stretched to embrace the rewarding gifts of the Blues. Triumphantly, he gave his greatest contribution in life through a different color than he innately possessed at birth.

Patrick Henry stretched beyond his innate personality to offer the "learned" Blue gifts in order to serve. In doing so, he chose the charactered path. In stretching, charactered people do not abandon their innate core motive or gifts. They simply use them to enhance their ability to enhance the lives of others. We must never take our innate gifts for granted. Yet, on the charactered path, we will be remembered best for the gifts we develop and freely give. Perhaps the reason lies in the charactered person's humble acceptance of the higher law, the optimum motive, and the courage to extend himself on behalf of his fellow human beings.

THE HEALTHY PATH

Anne—The European Contessa

Anne was a cherub: young, rotund, and very much alive. She found enjoyment in everything she experienced—as long as it didn't last very long. Anne came to me for clarity in understanding impulsive decisions she was making in her life and subsequent conflicts with her mother. She lived at home with her Red mother who could see no rhyme or reason for Anne's life, and who hoped somehow Anne could be convinced to take on her mother's responsible attitude toward daily survival.

Anne had no time for mere survival. She wanted to embrace life and "see it all." She longed to travel and meet new people. She longed to understand what made other cultures different from her own. She dreamed of being in the very places she had only read about. A healthy Yellow, Anne lived for the moment and found people easy to meet and enjoy.

We worked for some time on structure and boundaries. She learned to accept that her mother didn't have to understand her way of thinking or accept it. She discovered the importance of priorities and making responsible decisions based on what she values as well as on universal truths. Anne was growing up, but she maintained her innocent zest for living.

Within three months we had Anne back in school with renewed focus and higher expectations. She soon discovered that she could spend a semester abroad, fulfilling educational requirements at the same time as her own need for an exciting life. Within the year Anne had spent a semester in Europe and sailed halfway a round the world.

She embraced life with spirited anticipation. People welcomed her as they would a breath of fresh air. Meanwhile, her mother continued to dispel any notion of her success. Distraught that her daughter refused to accept the normal educational process, she could never accept Anne's unconventional approach. In her love for life and self, Anne learned to forgive her mother's lack of acceptance and simply sent her postcards from the numerous places she traveled.

True to her Yellow core, Anne experienced more excitement in one year than many people do in a lifetime. She risked much; she laughed often; she nonchalantly accepted her right to experience life differently than her mother. However, Anne never stretched to embrace the gifts of the other colors. Her life was lived exclusively in the domain of the Yellow core personality. She was healthy, considering how her focus was clearly on the Yellow strengths. Nonetheless, she saw life only through Yellow eyes. Her myopic orientation kept her limited to knowing only the "healthy" path.

THE UNHEALTHY PATH

White Flight

Recently I presented a seminar to business executives. One individual with a White personality bluntly rejected the concepts of *The Color Code,* seeing no beneficial application in his personal or professional life. Several participants offered him specific examples of how his White personality affected them in both positive and negative ways. I suggested thought and behavioral patterns he would most likely experience in conflict or stress situations due to his White personality. Silently, he stubbornly withdrew from any dialogue, resisting any further feedback or interaction with the group.

When the seminar concluded, we returned to our individual rooms prior to dinner. Returning thirty minutes later, the White executive and his wife (whom I had never met) entered the elevator I was on, already engaged in a conversation.

"I mean really," she complained, "how could anyone label the whole population into just four categories? And why would anyone want to be limited to just one personality anyway?!"

Her husband's eyes nervously darted between the lighted numbers on the elevator and the floor. Embarrassed at being caught, he suggested that they get off the elevator and take the stairs to the lobby.

Notably baffled, his wife said, "Are you crazy?!" (Guess her color!) "We're on the ninth floor. I'm not walking down nine flights of stairs. And besides," turning to look at me as if I were merely an innocent bystander, "there is plenty of room in this elevator."

This unhealthy White man preferred to justify his position behind my back rather than face me directly during the conference. This potentially candid and revealing encounter between his wife and me proved far too intense and problematic. They exited at the next floor with an outraged wife demanding that he remove his hand from her elbow and stop shoving her out the door. Rather than face me after being exposed for his unhealthy White antics, he avoided the conflict.

I sadly watched this man exit the elevator rather than face his limitations—limitations that will continue to haunt him and affect those with whom he interacts. How many lives could he have affirmed, how many people could he have assisted on their personal journey in life, had he been willing to see himself and accept the simple truths I came to share?

THE PATHOLOGICAL PATH

The Alcoholic and the Whiner

Jim was handsome, hard-working, and rich. He was also an alcoholic. Rene was beautiful, bored, vindictive, and a whiner. The one thing they had in common was their marriage license. The other was that they deserved each other. Yet, ironically, neither felt they deserved what they got.

Rene needed to commit somewhere and be accountable to someone other than herself and her husband. She needed a life. I recommended finding a job or getting involved with a charity. But she had no idea how to work and her favorite charity was herself, so she just looked busy and complained that Jim never came home. (Not an entirely *dumb* man, I might add.)

When Jim did come home, she complained about never going out. When they went out, she complained about never being home as a family. When they were together as a family, she complained about him being drunk too often.

However, the key to Jim's dysfunctional lifestyle was linked to his past. During one of our sessions, I discovered that he had attended West Point, but failed to make the cut. He arrived home early vowing never again to prove an embarrassment to his parents. He reluctantly accepted a dead-end position with the family corporation to appease them. He learned to hate his job, and eventually his wife, but refused to leave either one. Divorce was another embarrassment for the family he refused to even consider. Instead, he destroyed himself through alcohol and endless extramarital affairs. With age, his life became long on intrigue and short on substance.

Jim was a Blue man acting his life out in the limitations of a Red, and refusing to admit that the absence of purpose in his career and lack of intimacy at home was poisoning him. Rene was a White, acting with Blue limitations, and seeking solace in whining to friends and therapists—whomever would listen to the stories of her empty, tormented existence. Jim and Rene remained in mutual bondage to each other, complaining about how "unfair" life was and how "undeserving" they were to be stuck with each other.

They became victims of their own lies to themselves. They could not acknowledge their true core personalities, or take responsibility for living their lives within the limitations of other colors.

WRITE YOUR OWN EPITAPH

Whatever path you choose will have consequences. The higher the path, the greater the pain and the more satisfying the reward. You must decide what will be written on your tombstone. No one can walk your path. Only you can create it one step at a time. *Color Your Future* is for those caterpillars who have chosen to become what they were always meant to be—butterflies in flight.

The three essential tasks you must complete in order to transcend your caterpillar mentality are:

1. Accept your core personality and give your gifts freely.
2. Embrace the gifts offered by the other colors.
3. Master each of the six character building steps.

Membership in the charactered path can be extended only to those persistent individuals who seek this challenge with a humble heart, courageous commitment, and acceptance of grace. Their membership promises them fulfillment in flight.

CHAPTER TWO

The Hartman
Character Profile

The Hartman Personality Profile identifies your innate personality. Now we want to find out what "character accents" you have developed on the path to becoming charactered.

HARTMAN CHARACTER PROFILE

The Hartman Character Profile differs dramatically from the Hartman Personality Profile both in intent and administration. The Hartman Personality Profile is designed to verify one's core personality.* It is less concerned with the various color combinations reflected by your personality profile. The discovery of your innate core personality is its sole focus. You are allowed to select only one of four choices for each question in order to manifest your core personality.

The Hartman Character Profile is designed to identify your innate, *and developed* strengths and limitations from each of the four personality types. You will be asked to select five individuals to assist you. They will take the same profile on you that you take on yourself. Naturally the picture's accuracy depends on the integrity of those you select and your relationship with them. The administration of the profile calls for each word to be circled if it applies to how you are

---

*For more information on the Hartman Personality Profile, see my first book, *The Color Code*.

generally perceived "most of the time." Remember, we are seeking an accurate reading of where we are on our path to becoming charactered. The Hartman Personality Profile merely teaches us what kind of caterpillar we are. The Hartman Character Profile enlightens us as to where we are in our transition from caterpillar to butterfly.

Directions: 1): Review all the words in the top half of the profile first; 2): Consider each word as it relates to you in the various roles you play in life; 3): Circle those words that best characterize how you are most of the time; 4): Once you have completed the top half of the profile, follow the same directions for the bottom half of the profile. If you are completing the profile for someone else, please identify yourself by name and specify your relationship to the person for whom you are completing the profile.

Note: If you are having difficulty separating yourself in your various roles, you may want to make notes at the side of each word to specify if the word accurately portrays you only in a specific role (i.e., home, work, friends, etc.). *The profile is designed to help you find congruence in your life. If you find you have strong differences in your behavior at work and at home, you may be living separate lives and probably suffering from psychological incongruity.*

HARTMAN CHARACTER PROFILE EXAMPLES

Consider the following examples. Each of the individuals identified on the following profiles have Blue personalities. The results displayed on each profile indicate the individual's level (path) of spiritual-emotional-mental health. The concepts can easily by applied to each of the four personalities.

Example: "Charactered Blue"

HARTMAN CHARACTER PROFILE

A	B	C	D
decisive	intimate	peaceful	fun-loving
assertive	compassionate	tolerant	playful
action-oriented	sincere	kind	carefree
task-dominant	loyal	satisfied	enthusiastic
determined	thoughtful	even-tempered	optimistic
responsible	quality-oriented	agreeable	trusting
independent	well-mannered	patient	hopeful
logical	analytical	pleasant	happy
pragmatic	committed	accepting	charismatic
disciplined	dedicated	easy-going	sociable
confident	emotional	good listener	forgiving
powerful	dependable	inventive	spontaneous
leader	respectful	considerate	outgoing
productive	deliberate	diplomatic	lively
proactive	nurturing	adaptable	positive

E	F	G	H
selfish	worry prone	timid	uncommitted
insensitive	overly sensitive	directionless	self-centered
arrogant	self-righteous	indecisive	disorganized
critical of others	self-critical	unmotivated	irresponsible
always right	unforgiving	silently stubborn	undisciplined
impatient	judgmental	lazy	vain
calculating	suspicious	lackluster	afraid to face facts
intimidating	unrealistic expectations	indirect communicator	inconsistent
bossy	perfectionist	avoids conflict	unfocused
demanding	low self-esteem	self-deprecating	interruptive
argumentative	hard to please	indifferent	disruptive
aggressive	moody	ambivalent	impulsive
tactless	guilt prone	uninvolved	obnoxious
obsessive	jealous	unenthusiastic	naive

Directions: Highlight each of the words that best describes you or the individual for whom you are completing this profile.

Example: "Healthy Blue"

HARTMAN CHARACTER PROFILE

A	B	C	D
decisive	intimate	peaceful	fun-loving
assertive	compassionate	tolerant	playful
action-oriented	sincere	kind	carefree
task-dominant	loyal	satisfied	enthusiastic
determined	thoughtful	even-tempered	optimistic
responsible	quality-oriented	agreeable	trusting
independent	well-mannered	patient	hopeful
logical	analytical	pleasant	happy
pragmatic	committed	accepting	charismatic
disciplined	dedicated	easy-going	sociable
confident	emotional	good listener	forgiving
powerful	dependable	inventive	spontaneous
leader	respectful	considerate	outgoing
productive	deliberate	diplomatic	lively
proactive	nurturing	adaptable	positive

E	F	G	H
selfish	worry prone	timid	uncommitted
insensitive	overly sensitive	directionless	self-centered
arrogant	self-righteous	indecisive	disorganized
critical of others	self-critical	unmotivated	irresponsible
always right	unforgiving	silently stubborn	undisciplined
impatient	judgmental	lazy	vain
calculating	suspicious	lackluster	afraid to face facts
intimidating	unrealistic expectations	indirect communicator	inconsistent
bossy	perfectionist	avoids conflict	unfocused
demanding	low self-esteem	self-deprecating	interruptive
argumentative	hard to please	indifferent	disruptive
aggressive	moody	ambivalent	impulsive
tactless	guilt prone	uninvolved	obnoxious
obsessive	jealous	unenthusiastic	naive

Directions: Highlight each of the words that best describes you or the individual for whom you are completing this profile.

Example: "Unhealthy Blue"

HARTMAN CHARACTER PROFILE

A	B	C	D
decisive	intimate	peaceful	fun-loving
assertive	compassionate	tolerant	playful
action-oriented	sincere	kind	carefree
task-dominant	loyal	satisfied	enthusiastic
determined	thoughtful	even-tempered	optimistic
responsible	quality-oriented	agreeable	trusting
independent	well-mannered	patient	hopeful
logical	analytical	pleasant	happy
pragmatic	committed	accepting	charismatic
disciplined	dedicated	easy-going	sociable
confident	emotional	good listener	forgiving
powerful	dependable	inventive	spontaneous
leader	respectful	considerate	outgoing
productive	deliberate	diplomatic	lively
proactive	nurturing	adaptable	positive

E	F	G	H
selfish	worry prone	timid	uncommitted
insensitive	overly sensitive	directionless	self-centered
arrogant	self-righteous	indecisive	disorganized
critical of others	self-critical	unmotivated	irresponsible
always right	unforgiving	silently stubborn	undisciplined
impatient	judgmental	lazy	vain
calculating	suspicious	lackluster	afraid to face facts
intimidating	unrealistic expectations	indirect communicator	inconsistent
bossy	perfectionist	avoids conflict	unfocused
demanding	low self-esteem	self-deprecating	interruptive
argumentative	hard to please	indifferent	disruptive
aggressive	moody	ambivalent	impulsive
tactless	guilt prone	uninvolved	obnoxious
obsessive	jealous	unenthusiastic	naive

Directions: Highlight each of the words that best describes you or the individual for whom you are completing this profile.

Example: "Sick Blue"

HARTMAN CHARACTER PROFILE

A	B	C	D
decisive	intimate	peaceful	fun-loving
assertive	compassionate	tolerant	playful
action-oriented	sincere	kind	carefree
task-dominant	loyal	satisfied	enthusiastic
determined	thoughtful	even-tempered	optimistic
responsible	quality-oriented	agreeable	trusting
independent	well-mannered	patient	hopeful
logical	analytical	pleasant	happy
pragmatic	committed	accepting	charismatic
disciplined	dedicated	easy-going	sociable
confident	emotional	good listener	forgiving
powerful	dependable	inventive	spontaneous
leader	respectful	considerate	outgoing
productive	deliberate	diplomatic	lively
proactive	nurturing	adaptable	positive

E	F	G	H
selfish	worry prone	timid	uncommitted
insensitive	overly sensitive	directionless	self-centered
arrogant	self-righteous	indecisive	disorganized
critical of others	self-critical	unmotivated	irresponsible
always right	unforgiving	silently stubborn	undisciplined
impatient	judgmental	lazy	vain
calculating	suspicious	lackluster	afraid to face facts
intimidating	unrealistic expectations	indirect communicator	inconsistent
bossy	perfectionist	avoids conflict	unfocused
demanding	low self-esteem	self-deprecating	interruptive
argumentative	hard to please	indifferent	disruptive
aggressive	moody	ambivalent	impulsive
tactless	guilt prone	uninvolved	obnoxious
obsessive	jealous	unenthusiastic	naive

Directions: Highlight each of the words that best describes you or the individual for whom you are completing this profile.

Self On Self

HARTMAN CHARACTER PROFILE

A	B	C	D
decisive	intimate	peaceful	fun-loving
assertive	compassionate	tolerant	playful
action-oriented	sincere	kind	carefree
task-dominant	loyal	satisfied	enthusiastic
determined	thoughtful	even-tempered	optimistic
responsible	quality-oriented	agreeable	trusting
independent	well-mannered	patient	hopeful
logical	analytical	pleasant	happy
pragmatic	committed	accepting	charismatic
disciplined	dedicated	easy-going	sociable
confident	emotional	good listener	forgiving
powerful	dependable	inventive	spontaneous
leader	respectful	considerate	outgoing
productive	deliberate	diplomatic	lively
proactive	nurturing	adaptable	positive

E	F	G	H
selfish	worry prone	timid	uncommitted
insensitive	overly sensitive	directionless	self-centered
arrogant	self-righteous	indecisive	disorganized
critical of others	self-critical	unmotivated	irresponsible
always right	unforgiving	silently stubborn	undisciplined
impatient	judgmental	lazy	vain
calculating	suspicious	lackluster	afraid to face facts
intimidating	unrealistic expectations	indirect	inconsistent communicator
bossy	perfectionist	avoids conflict	unfocused
demanding	low self-esteem	self-deprecating	interruptive
argumentative	hard to please	indifferent	disruptive
aggressive	moody	ambivalent	impulsive
tactless	guilt prone	uninvolved	obnoxious
obsessive	jealous	unenthusiastic	naive

Directions: Highlight each of the words that best describes you or the individual for whom you are completing this profile most of the time.

Spouse/Child On Self

HARTMAN CHARACTER PROFILE

A	B	C	D
decisive	intimate	peaceful	fun-loving
assertive	compassionate	tolerant	playful
action-oriented	sincere	kind	carefree
task-dominant	loyal	satisfied	enthusiastic
determined	thoughtful	even-tempered	optimistic
responsible	quality-oriented	agreeable	trusting
independent	well-mannered	patient	hopeful
logical	analytical	pleasant	happy
pragmatic	committed	accepting	charismatic
disciplined	dedicated	easy-going	sociable
confident	emotional	good listener	forgiving
powerful	dependable	inventive	spontaneous
leader	respectful	considerate	outgoing
productive	deliberate	diplomatic	lively
proactive	nurturing	adaptable	positive
E	F	G	H
selfish	worry prone	timid	uncommitted
insensitive	overly sensitive	directionless	self-centered
arrogant	self-righteous	indecisive	disorganized
critical of others	self-critical	unmotivated	irresponsible
always right	unforgiving	silently stubborn	undisciplined
impatient	judgmental	lazy	vain
calculating	suspicious	lackluster	afraid to face facts
intimidating	unrealistic expectations	indirect	inconsistent communicator
bossy	perfectionist	avoids conflict	unfocused
demanding	low self-esteem	self-deprecating	interruptive
argumentative	hard to please	indifferent	disruptive
aggressive	moody	ambivalent	impulsive
tactless	guilt prone	uninvolved	obnoxious
obsessive	jealous	unenthusiastic	naive

Directions: Highlight each of the words that best describes you or the individual for whom you are completing this profile most of the time.

Friend On Self

HARTMAN CHARACTER PROFILE

A	B	C	D
decisive	intimate	peaceful	fun-loving
assertive	compassionate	tolerant	playful
action-oriented	sincere	kind	carefree
task-dominant	loyal	satisfied	enthusiastic
determined	thoughtful	even-tempered	optimistic
responsible	quality-oriented	agreeable	trusting
independent	well-mannered	patient	hopeful
logical	analytical	pleasant	happy
pragmatic	committed	accepting	charismatic
disciplined	dedicated	easy-going	sociable
confident	emotional	good listener	forgiving
powerful	dependable	inventive	spontaneous
leader	respectful	considerate	outgoing
productive	deliberate	diplomatic	lively
proactive	nurturing	adaptable	positive

E	F	G	H
selfish	worry prone	timid	uncommitted
insensitive	overly sensitive	directionless	self-centered
arrogant	self-righteous	indecisive	disorganized
critical of others	self-critical	unmotivated	irresponsible
always right	unforgiving	silently stubborn	undisciplined
impatient	judgmental	lazy	vain
calculating	suspicious	lackluster	afraid to face facts
intimidating	unrealistic expectations	indirect communicator	inconsistent
bossy	perfectionist	avoids conflict	unfocused
demanding	low self-esteem	self-deprecating	interruptive
argumentative	hard to please	indifferent	disruptive
aggressive	moody	ambivalent	impulsive
tactless	guilt prone	uninvolved	obnoxious
obsessive	jealous	unenthusiastic	naive

Directions: Highlight each of the words that best describes you or the individual for whom you are completing this profile most of the time.

Friend On Self

HARTMAN CHARACTER PROFILE

A	B	C	D
decisive	intimate	peaceful	fun-loving
assertive	compassionate	tolerant	playful
action-oriented	sincere	kind	carefree
task-dominant	loyal	satisfied	enthusiastic
determined	thoughtful	even-tempered	optimistic
responsible	quality-oriented	agreeable	trusting
independent	well-mannered	patient	hopeful
logical	analytical	pleasant	happy
pragmatic	committed	accepting	charismatic
disciplined	dedicated	easy-going	sociable
confident	emotional	good listener	forgiving
powerful	dependable	inventive	spontaneous
leader	respectful	considerate	outgoing
productive	deliberate	diplomatic	lively
proactive	nurturing	adaptable	positive

E	F	G	H
selfish	worry prone	timid	uncommitted
insensitive	overly sensitive	directionless	self-centered
arrogant	self-righteous	indecisive	disorganized
critical of others	self-critical	unmotivated	irresponsible
always right	unforgiving	silently stubborn	undisciplined
impatient	judgmental	lazy	vain
calculating	suspicious	lackluster	afraid to face facts
intimidating	unrealistic expectations	indirect communicator	inconsistent
bossy	perfectionist	avoids conflict	unfocused
demanding	low self-esteem	self-deprecating	interruptive
argumentative	hard to please	indifferent	disruptive
aggressive	moody	ambivalent	impulsive
tactless	guilt prone	uninvolved	obnoxious
obsessive	jealous	unenthusiastic	naive

Directions: Highlight each of the words that best describes you or the individual for whom you are completing this profile most of the time.

Work Colleague On Self

HARTMAN CHARACTER PROFILE

A	B	C	D
decisive	intimate	peaceful	fun-loving
assertive	compassionate	tolerant	playful
action-oriented	sincere	kind	carefree
task-dominant	loyal	satisfied	enthusiastic
determined	thoughtful	even-tempered	optimistic
responsible	quality-oriented	agreeable	trusting
independent	well-mannered	patient	hopeful
logical	analytical	pleasant	happy
pragmatic	committed	accepting	charismatic
disciplined	dedicated	easy-going	sociable
confident	emotional	good listener	forgiving
powerful	dependable	inventive	spontaneous
leader	respectful	considerate	outgoing
productive	deliberate	diplomatic	lively
proactive	nurturing	adaptable	positive

E	F	G	H
selfish	worry prone	timid	uncommitted
insensitive	overly sensitive	directionless	self-centered
arrogant	self-righteous	indecisive	disorganized
critical of others	self-critical	unmotivated	irresponsible
always right	unforgiving	silently stubborn	undisciplined
impatient	judgmental	lazy	vain
calculating	suspicious	lackluster	afraid to face facts
intimidating	unrealistic expectations	indirect communicator	inconsistent
bossy	perfectionist	avoids conflict	unfocused
demanding	low self-esteem	self-deprecating	interruptive
argumentative	hard to please	indifferent	disruptive
aggressive	moody	ambivalent	impulsive
tactless	guilt prone	uninvolved	obnoxious
obsessive	jealous	unenthusiastic	naive

Directions: Highlight each of the words that best describes you or the individual for whom you are completing this profile most of the time.

In reviewing your profile results, you will undoubtedly have numerous questions; questions, perhaps, of differences in how you scored yourself and how others perceived you; questions about why you have circled numerous adjectives in some categories and relatively few in others; questions about whether your childhood or your current career orientation influence your answers. Sorting through the Hartman Character Profile requires the humility to face ourselves as we are, the vision to see what we hope to become, and the courage to bring them together.

HARTMAN CHARACTER PROFILE REVIEW

Step One. Place all the completed profiles on you in front of you. Review the words you and others selected in the various columns. The columns are marked A to D in strengths and E to H in limitations. The A column represents Red strengths, while the E column reflects Red limitations. The B column is Blue strengths and "F" column is Blue limitations. The column labeled C represents White strengths, and the G column reflects White limitations. The "D" column represents Yellow strengths and H column reflects Yellow limitations.

Step Two. If possible, it is helpful to compare your scores from the Hartman Personality Profile with your responses to the Hartman Character Profile. Typically your innate core personality determined by the personality profile is validated by reflecting the most responses in the same color column on the character profile as well. For example, if your predominant color on the personality profile is Blue, you will most likely find your greatest number of responses on the character profile in the Blue column as well.

Step Three. Review your strengths in *all* columns. How balanced have you become in life? Becoming charactered requires that we discover our innate core personality and be true to it. Simultaneously, however, we must seek to develop the gifts of the other colors and integrate them as genuine dimensions of our "charactered" selves. A healthy individual will reflect a major concentration of responses on the Hartman Character Profile in his/her innate color's column, while a "charactered" individual will find a much broader blending of gifts across the entire top half of the profile.

Step Four. Review your limitations in all categories. Where are your weaknesses? Which limitations are chosen most often in your eyes and the eyes of others? Your limitations will haunt you and deny you access to a charactered life. For example, if your core personality is Red and you (and or your selected evaluators) have circled numerous words in the Blue limitations F column, you are essentially sabotaging yourself. Society expects leadership and assertiveness from you. If you are a Red core personality motivated by power yet suffer from Blue limitations of perfectionism, bearing grudges, and self-righteousness, you will not be respected or followed. People are confused by your double messages sent by Red strengths and Blue limitations.

In becoming charactered, first eliminate your Blue limitations. *We are much more tolerant of limitations displayed within one's core personality than those weaknesses which belong to another personality type.* People are generally confused and angered by displayed limitations which are foreign to your innate core personality.

The Hartman Character Profile is your compass and accurately pinpoints where you are on your path toward taking flight. Characteristically, the column displaying your lowest amount of strengths and limitations is the personality you struggle understanding most. Developing strengths from their color will validate them as well as helping you acknowledge their value. In turn, they often appreciate your efforts to develop their strengths, which enhances mutual admiration and respect.

Step Five. Review each of the Hartman Character Profiles filled out on your behalf. Consider how they differ and how they resemble each other. What do the collective results tell you? For example, if a man is more highly regarded by his business associates than his wife, he should consider whether he is different at home than at work. If he is presenting his best self on the job, he can expect to receive higher marks at work than at home. He may need to reprioritize where he places his energy in life. Perhaps he suffers from personal fears and inadequacies that do not affect his professional relationships. Another consideration is the nature of his wife. Is she capable of valuing him or will she never be satisfied? He should ask her specifically what attributes he displays that cause her to respond to his profile as she does.

(Note: Always seek feedback when possible from the source of your profile. It can help to clarify the intention of their selected responses. Others' feedback will help you gain valuable perceptions essential to making the difficult changes ahead on your path toward the charactered life.)

Step Six. After reviewing and discussing your character profiles, select three words from the limitations columns that describe you and which you find most inhibiting of a quality life. Now search each of the strengths columns (A to D) for three positive traits that are opposites of your selected limitations. You will most likely find these strengths in columns other than your innate personality. *Ironically, your success in becoming charactered depends entirely on your ability to discover and nurture gifts from the other colors. Commit to work on these selected strengths for one year, or until someone compliments you on your ability to display them.*

Seek role models who were born with these gifts. Better yet, acknowledge charactered individuals who have gone before you in stretching to develop the very gifts you seek. Focus on these gifts. Breathe life into them. Challenge yourself to integrate them into your natural personality. Use the six steps in this book to help you on your path. *Color Your Future* provides a general map but you must define your specific way. Enjoy the magic of all you were born to become.

GLOSSARY OF PROFILE TERMS

Accepting: welcoming, receiving, agreeing

Adaptable: changeable, adjustable, versatile

Aggressive: forward, pushy, selfish, versatile

Agreeable: good-natured, pleasant, content, congenial

Argumentative: quarrelsome, contentious, antagonistic

Ambivalent: uncertain, undecided, "I don't care" attitude

Analytical: complex reasoning, organized, systematic, careful

Arrogant: conceited, egotistical, air of superiority

Assertive: direct, to the point, outspoken, determined

Bossy: pushy, overbearing, domineering, dictatorial

Calculating: cunning, scheming, shrewd, manipulative

Carefree: lighthearted, untroubled, without worry

Charismatic: charming, magnetic, captivating, appealing

Committed: dedicated, dependable, loyal, faithful

Compassionate: caring, empathetic, considerate, charitable

Confident: self-assured, poised, belief in one's ability

Considerate: kind, thoughtful, remembering

Decisive: determined, conclusive, able to act

Dedicated: emotionally committed, devoted, loyal, faithful

Deliberate: purposeful, reflective, contemplative

Demanding: pressuring, commanding, "You will!" versus "Will you?"

Dependable: reliable, responsible, trustworthy

Determined: firm, resolute, doesn't give up

Diplomatic: tactful, discreet, concern for mutual agreement

Directionless: without aim or direction

Disciplined: self-controlled, restrained, not impulsive

Disorganized: disorderly, haphazard, unsystematic

Disruptive: disturbing, provoking, agitating, interrupting

Easygoing: laid back, relaxed, uncomplicated, mellow

Emotional: not logical, think from the heart, feelings are the priority

Enthusiastic: eager, spirited, energetic, excited

Even tempered: easy going, calm, not excitable or easily ruffled

Forgiving: quick to excuse self and others

Fun loving: enjoys the moment, playful, happy

Guilt prone: quick to feel or take unrealistic blame or feel shame

Idealistic: see and want the best in others and life

Impatient: restless, hasty, hurried, intolerant

Impulsive: unpredictable, hasty, don't think before acting

Inconsistent: unpredictable, erratic, not stable, variable

Indecisive: uncertain, hesitant, ambivalent, can't decide

Independent: self-reliant, autonomous, self-sufficient

Indifferent: apathetic, unconcerned, emotionally detached

Insensitive: limited compassion, unfeeling

Interrupter: begin speaking before someone is finished

Intimidate: to make others feel insecure

Intimate: the desire for close associations or contacts with others

Inventive: creative, imaginative, sees possibilities with unusual perspective

Jealous: envious, covetous

Judgmental: critical, fault-finding

Kind: gentile, pleasant, good natured, considerate

Lackluster: dull, boring, without enthusiasm

Lazy: inactive, passive, idle, sluggish

Logical: rational, reasonable, obvious

Loyal: dependable, faithful, true, reliable, committed

Merciless: insensitive, callous, heartless, ruthless

Moody: sulky, temperamental, emotional highs and lows

Naive: trusting, gullible, unsuspecting

Nurturing: caring, concerned, attentive

Obsessive: preoccupation with ideas, people, emotions, and behaviors

Obnoxious: irritating, annoying

Opinionated: strong feelings about ideas and beliefs

Optimistic: cheerful, hopeful, idealistic

Outgoing: friendly, sociable, gregarious

Passive: submissive, compliant, nonresistant

Patient: tolerant, accepting, understanding

Peaceful: calm, quiet, serene, gentle, tranquil

Perfectionist: performance without mistake, error or defect

Playful: fun loving, merry, amusing, entertaining

Pleasant: enjoyable, pleasing, agreeable, likable

Powerful: authoritative, influential, commanding, ability to perform efficiently

Pragmatic: practical, realistic, workable

Productive: efficient, resourceful, constructive

Quality-oriented: desires excellence and accuracy

Reliable: dependable, responsible, faithful

Reluctant: hesitant, reserved, timid, restrained

Respectful: polite, gracious, courteous, considerate

Self-centered: concerned mainly with self

Self-critical: self-deprecating, find fault with self

Self-deprecating: sees self in unrealistic and negative view, refuse to accept self

Self-righteous: morally judgmental, "holier than thou" attitude

Selfish: primary concern for self above that of others

Sensitive: Concerned with others, aware of emotions and needs

Silently stubborn: quietly inflexible, unyielding, obstinate

Sincere: genuine, true, trustworthy

Sociable: friendly, outgoing, gregarious

Spontaneous: unplanned, impulsive, unrehearsed, risking

Suspicious: distrustful, skeptical, wary

Tactless: rude, thoughtless, inconsiderate

Thoughtful: considerate, attentive, concerned, caring, thinks of others

Timid: shy, bashful, unassertive, quiet, reserved

Tolerant: accepting, understanding, open minded

Trusting: believing, not suspicious, seeing the good

Uncommitted: unwilling to commit, flighty, disloyal

Undisciplined: not in control, unrestrained, indulgent

Unenthusiastic: not excited, does not display eagerness to be involved

Unfocused: easily distracted, unable to concentrate

Unforgiving: to hold a grudge, emotionally unyielding

Unmotivated: not easily moved to action, inactive, uninspired

Vain: conceited, self-centered, self-admiring, egotistical

Worry-prone: inclined to be upset or fret easily

CHAPTER THREE

Butterflies

If you were accused of being a successful person, would there be enough evidence to convict you?

Becoming charactered is the ultimate human experience. No financial reward or fame can touch the grandeur of this process. Charactered lives are rare. However, it is not their rarity that attracts us. Rather, we are mesmerized by the personal power displayed by charactered people. Their power is derived from the simple truths that center their lives.

To become charactered, we must successfully master psycho-social-spiritual health. We cannot substitute other steps, such as social skills or physical fitness, to replace these. *Color Your Future* is your guide through the six steps of mastering psycho-social-spiritual health.

For me, your success as a human being can be measured best by whether or not you can be trusted.

CAN YOU BE TRUSTED TO . . .
Value yourself (step one)?
Seek universal truth (step two)?
Have clean motives (step three)?
Focus your commitments (step four)?
Discover balance (step five)?
Serve others (step six)?

Charactered people seek affirmative answers to these six questions throughout their life. Earning trust in all six dimensions is the test of charactered individuals. These six steps are dedicated to helping you discover all you were born to become.

GIFTS FOR YOUR JOURNEY

On your journey, accept three essential gifts that you must carry with you. These gifts are *humility, courage,* and *patience.* Each of the six steps is difficult. As the actor Robert Blake once said, "God don't give no points for doing something you ain't afraid to do."

Stretching to master some steps will prove more difficult than others. To be successful you must transcend fear and embrace love. Building a charactered foundation through mastery of each step secures a quality life. Like taking a fast roller-coaster ride, the charactered path is filled with rewarding ups and terrifying downs. On this path, we experience the exhilaration of being fully trusted, fully human, and fully alive.

HUMILITY

Humility is learning one's true place in the universe and his or her relationship with others. We have distinct value because we are human beings with minds to comprehend and hearts to feel the essence of life. However, we are not perfect; we must accept our innate limitations and seek others' help in experiencing the life we have been given.

Picture humility as symbolized by water. Without it, we die. Without it, all other gifts have only limited meaning. Humility grants us access to wisdom and quality relationships. Without it, we become intellectually brittle and emotionally hardened.

The opposite of humility is insecurity. Insecure people hide from themselves and others' criticism. Struggling to even accept themselves as they are, they have no use for the close scrutiny of others. They simply refuse to invite feedback from others, denying themselves the personal development necessary to becoming charactered. Like frightened children, they cut themselves off from others, becoming like isolated ponds, and eventually dying from lack of outside nutrients and essential life-affirming connections.

Insecure people mask their fears in two predominant styles. Reds and

Yellows usually prefer to hide behind arrogance, while Blues and Whites typically prefer to whine about their inadequacy. Ironically, each resents the other's style. Yet, they are both merely masks for the same fear.

Humility requires us to remove our masks and expose our vulnerabilities so that we can learn all we can, and love all we can. Humble people revere life and human dignity. They never want to block another's progress or impede another's journey. Yet we are all born with natural limitations. Herein lies the paradox: We may not want to hurt someone else, but if we don't overcome these natural limitations, we will, indeed, do damage.

ROLE MODELS AND MENTORS

Humility allows us to seek mentors and role models for overcoming our limitations. Role models live their lives comfortably and effortlessly in strengths where we know only limitation. For example, you may be promoted to a leadership position at work but lack the strength of assertion. As a charactered individual, you would recognize your limitation and seek out someone who has a strength in the area of "assertiveness." This strength most commonly lies with the Red personality. Watch how Reds think and react to situations and learn from them how to most effectively apply the gift of assertiveness. Whenever possible, tell them you have selected them as a role model for the specific trait you are learning. It gives them a well-deserved compliment and will enhance their respect for you.

Mentors play a different role in your character development. They will be extremely helpful in teaching you how to embrace the strength because they had to walk the same path you are now embracing. Mentors are usually more helpful in teaching you the basic strategies for change than role models who came by their gift innately. Role models are usually better players than coaches because they don't know how they do the trait so well; they just do it. Role models are helpful because they exude the quality of life you can enjoy once you embrace their gift.

Charactered and healthy individuals are capable of being both mentors and role models because they either have developed the strengths of other colors or simply demonstrate the gifts of their own color. Everyone can use both mentors and role models. Consider for a minute a personality limitation you have that would benefit your life to replace with a strength of another personality. Now think about a person who demonstrates that strength and someone who has developed that strength you now seek. Congratulations: the humble individual has already begun his journey.

COURAGE

Courage is the price one pays for peace.
—AMELIA EARHART

There are no easy paths to becoming charactered. *Every time I watch a patient truly embrace the charactered path, I am in awe.* To see them take their first steps is no less magical than watching a baby learn to walk. Innocently trusting, she risks becoming a fool; she risks inevitable rejection and painful moments of discovery.

At a retreat, Elaine (a deeply wounded Blue) and I shared a role play about her rejection by her mother. Having been passed to her grandparents by her mother for child care, Elaine felt abandoned. She visited her mother several years later hoping to restore a familial bond. While Elaine was visiting, guests surprised them, and her mother quickly requested that Elaine represent herself as her mother's sister, rather than her daughter.

"No one knows about you," the mother (a pathological White personality) explained. "It would just make it easier for me. You understand."

Elaine understood all too well. She had always been an inconvenience to her mother. This rejection had plagued her her entire life. At the retreat, she faced her greatest fear.

"How can I love this woman who has continually refused to love me?" she asked.

Months of courageous personal development prepared her to walk through the pain of accepting her mother's rejection. We all wept as we witnessed this frightened woman face her mother (played by me) only to be rebuffed by her mother's inability to love. This time, however, Elaine would not be denied her right to love her mother.

Following the retreat, she visited her mother again. She asked for nothing but the chance to love this woman, who had, for so long, refused to love her. She called frequently and sent gifts of personal value. No longer a victim of her bitter emotional rejection, Elaine displayed a hero's courage. She came bearing gifts of love with no strings attached; no expectations, no demands. Freely and consistently she loved her mother until one day, more than a year later, this poem from her mother arrived in the mail.

MY TREASURE FOUND

Oh little one
Oh precious child of mine
I touch your raven hair
And watch those brown eyes shine.

The years have passed and I
was gone.
I mourn the years, I missed
so much.

I wasn't there and I was wrong.
It's really hard to just forget
the past, the years that I
regret.

But little one, my now grown
child,
You've made me proud, you're
worth the pain
My time, now short, is filled
with you.

The past is gone
you're here again.

My precious treasure found.

I love you Elaine,

MOTHER

Like Elaine, we must show courage in pursuing these six steps of character building. The arduous path demands that no one experience its exquisite truths except those who have a courageous and humble heart.

PATIENCE

The gift of patience requires exactly that: patience. We cannot make it happen. We must simply invite its presence and find room for it when it decides to visit our lives.

Any individual who has struggled to trade one of his innate personality limitations for another personality's natural strengths will attest to the importance of having patience. I worked on being "thoughtful" for an entire year (and you Blues are all out there saying to yourselves, "What's so difficult about being thoughtful? For me that's like slipping on a pair of comfortable shoes."), and it was like putting on water skis while in a lake with the wind blowing and the rain pelting my face. It just didn't come naturally. But for you Blues, who think being thoughtful is simple, try waking up every day happy and never worrying about anything. Now we're into some serious Yellow territory: Happy and carefree—now it feels like I'm slipping on a pair of comfortable shoes! (Any of you Blues struggling with your skis yet?)

Give the process of becoming charactered some time. Great things take time and we should afford ourselves time to evolve. Patience, however, does not mean avoidance, or procrastination. Patience specifically refers to the attitude one takes toward the process of embracing, completing, and becoming charactered.

Decide on the steps of becoming charactered you need most in your life. Determine what personality limitations restrict your life most and find a mentor and role model to help you free yourself. To become trusted by others is a process that gives life its greatest meaning. *Be patient with yourself and those around you who struggle to find their way.* As M. Scott Peck says in the first line of his powerful book *The Road Less Traveled,* "Life is difficult."

CHAPTER FOUR

Step One: Value Yourself

If I am not for myself, who will be for me?
—Hillel

IT AIN'T EASY BEIN' GREEN

One recent morning was unusually cool and moist. I was outside enjoying my garden when I noticed a little green frog. He looked rather pale, as though he might be sick. I picked him up and asked him (you know we shrinks will talk to anyone), "What's the matter with you, little frog?"

Suddenly I realized that he wasn't physically sick at all. Big teardrops fell from his bulging eyes.

He blinked at me and said, "Ribett! Sometimes I think it would be much nicer being a different color. I'd like to be noticed, like the roses in the garden or the sun on the water or the moon in the night sky"

I stroked his green back and said, "But green is the color of spring. It's the color of grass and leaves and shamrocks. It can be big like the ocean or imposing like the mountains."

"Hey," he perked up. "I never thought of green that way before. Thanks for the chat. I think I understand what you mean. I'm green and I should like it. And I do! And besides, money's green. Ribett! Ribett!"

My conversation with the little frog never happened, of course. Yet symbolically it has happened thousands of times with people struggling to accept and value themselves simply as they are. Perhaps they feel stupid, or financially strapped, or unpopular. Some feel inadequate at work, while others feel a sense of failure at home.

Most people simply are not content being themselves. They expend endless energy, often in anger, seeking new direction to their lives or desperately demanding that others approve of them, the very person *they* cannot accept themselves. Some are consumed with bitterness and resentment toward dysfunctional relationships or unmet expectations; some are angry with others for controlling their lives.

Unlike nature, where rocks accept that they are not trees, and rivers willingly flow, many human beings challenge their identity, making it difficult to value themselves simply as they are.

Self-acceptance begins with self-identity. The question of self-esteem, posed so long ago by Hillel, "If I am not for myself, who will be for me?" proffers no easy answer. Everyone can find self-esteem at some point in life; the key is perpetuating the gift beyond the moment so that its inviting joy can be relished and shared with others who pursue the answer to the question.

The Color Code provides ample insights for self-realization. We must be humble in order to accurately identify our innate strengths and limitations. Color coding truths begin the process of self-esteem by clarifying our unique roles and gifts we bring to this universe.

Step one in *Color Your Future* focuses on the second stage of developing self-esteem, which is learning to value and accept ourselves and our gifts. Once we accept ourselves for who we are, we are more inclined to share ourselves with others. When we genuinely value ourselves, we are able to share—and sharing brings the intimacy to service.

The ultimate motive that drives charactered individuals is the desire and ability to serve. Without the interest or capacity to assist others, there is no point in walking the charactered path.

WHAT DOES IT MEAN TO VALUE YOURSELF?

Self-esteem is simply accepting ourselves as we are rather than demanding we be all we are capable of becoming. *We must learn to value our basic package of who we are simply because we breathe.*

Self-esteem has nothing to do with achieving or producing or even becoming. Rather, it is that all-encompassing sensation of feeling acceptable, capable, and most of all lovable, simply because we are alive. It has everything to do with accepting ourselves and appreciating who we are. The optimum motive of service begins by serving ourselves. We must have genuine compassion for the personality we were born with.

The first moments when we begin to evaluate ourselves can be terrifying. There are no airs to put on. There are no facades to hide behind. There are no defense mechanisms to ease the fear. There is only you, confronted by yourself; your own thoughts and your own actions.

It's ironic that we must like ourselves well enough to accept not liking some of the things that we find. Depressed people have the most difficulty with this. Fearing they will not discover any positive aspects in themselves, they often resist hearing feedback, either positive or negative. Honestly seeing ourselves for who we are is like giving birth—painful and frightening, yet passionate and very life affirming. This is when the process of becoming charactered actually begins.

Your first examination might take a few hours or days; it might take weeks or months, depending on the individual. The Hartman Personality Profile can assist you in this examination as long as you give accurate and honest answers. The realization that you are a Red, Blue, White, or Yellow, complete with unique motives, needs, and wants, can give you tremendous insight into yourself.

The danger lies not in our innate, core motives, but rather in their excesses. Power motivates Reds. They seek production. When they manipulate people in order to accomplish their selfish desires, they are practicing excess. When Blues browbeat another in self-righteous indignation for a perceived infraction of their rules, they are practicing excess. When Whites quietly sulk because they have things to say but are unwilling to pay the price, they are practicing excess. When Yellows don't show up for work just because they would rather be sailing or betting a long shot at the track, they are practicing excess. The charactered path teaches us methods for maintaining moderation in all things. We must learn to accept ourselves and reject our excesses.

I remember watching Kit, an excessive Blue, middle-aged patient who was struggling to accept herself. Each session seemed like a battle of wills. I was terribly direct and she was terribly offended, but neither would give up on our joint venture. She would verbally attack her White husband on a daily basis for his "obvious" limitations. She was convinced that her children would never reach their potential. What she was really saying was that she didn't like, or accept, herself and consequently couldn't like, or accept, anyone else.

Slowly we built a foundation upon which she could value herself. As she warmed to the idea that she could actually like who she was, Kit found value in her husband and children too. After several years, I literally ran into her on the ski slopes. She looked younger than ever. Happy and accepting of herself and her life, she had learned to accept the choices her family made as well. She loved them whether or not their choices matched hers.

It was tax season and her husband, Joe, was chained to his desk. "Remember how I used to whine and nag him about working so much," she reflected. "Well, this year I just packed all the kids in the car and we drove to Colorado to see Jennifer, who is attending college in Boulder. They love to snow ski and I love to watch them. We're having such fun.

"I wish my husband could be here," she continued, "but I have learned to love him for his dependability and job security. Remember how I used to beat him up so I wouldn't have to look at myself? What a waste of a life. I was really cheating both of us, wasn't I? And the kids, too, for that matter. Well, I don't do that anymore. Life's too short for that nonsense. The most ironic part is that things really haven't changed that much since the first time I saw you, but now I'm having such a great time with myself and the very people I used to resent. How could I have been so wrong about us when actually we're all pretty good stuff?!"

Kit learned about self-esteem from me. I learned about this gift from a woman I never actually met. Her story came to me through a patient who shared some time with her when they both lived in Northern California, several years back.

THE BEACHED WHALE

"We would always go skinny-dipping in the river," my patient said. "A group of friends would pack a picnic and spend the day together.

What fun we had! My best girlfriend was rotund and looked like a beached whale all sprawled out on the riverbank. Her boyfriend was gorgeous. He looked like a model. So good-looking.

"And this woman never worried about him with other women. She was never concerned with his getting second looks from other women. No jealousy. No fear. Just this marvelous beached whale propped up on a pillow and laughing up a storm, swapping jokes, and inviting delightful conversation. She absolutely loved people, and she absolutely adored herself. For the life of me, I don't know why. To look at her, you certainly wouldn't think she had any reason to!"

Her last sentence struck me like a bolt of lightning: *She adored herself for no apparent reason.*

"That's it! That's it!" I said. *"That* is true self-esteem!"

I felt as if I had discovered gold. What a rich insight into one of the greatest maladies of our time. She didn't value herself because of anything she produced, how she looked, or anyone she knew. She liked herself simply because she *breathed.* No expectations are required to be a member of the human race. In fact, with regard to true self-esteem, expectations are a hinderance. *Simply breathing is our standing invitation to value ourselves.*

HOW DO YOU KNOW
IF YOU VALUE YOURSELF?

Each color brings a different perspective on self-esteem. Reds often feel that they are only as good as their last game. Blues struggle with an overabundance of guilt and self-flagellation for not measuring up to unrealistic expectations. Whites usually pay a high personal price in order to preserve an atmosphere of peace which they need to feel comfortable. Yellows generally find ways to value themselves and get others to do so as well. Yellows typically bring the gift of self-esteem to the smorgasbord of life.

Self-esteem is not just words, or even actions, it is an *attitude;* one that says I have worth simply because I am a human being; simply because I breathe and I am alive. People with self-value accept themselves. They don't expect.

THE SERENDIPITY OF FEELING GOOD
ABOUT YOURSELF

Charactered individuals live for the present, unconcerned with the fears of tomorrow or regrets of the past. They quickly slot themselves into playful adventures, free of negative strings and rigid boundaries. Like children, all colors would benefit by learning to "seize the moments" life offers. The Romans even had a term for this; "carpe diem," meaning "seize the day." With time, these singular moments reward us with memories of a quality life.

TRAINS, BOATS, AND PLANES

Many of us get on trains, boats, and planes with the singular purpose of getting off. From the minute we board, we are impatiently waiting to arrive at our destination. Meanwhile, we miss so many wonderful experiences—beautiful sunsets, festive foods, and fascinating people. We don't take the time to look because we are preoccupied with our arrival. We can't be concerned with eating because we are obsessed with how we will look when we get there. We are so absorbed with how we will enjoy our lives once we arrive at our destination, that we are often oblivious to the people who surround us.

"When we get off the plane," we think.

"When we close one last business deal," we promise.

"When our children are reared and gone," we plan.

"When we have more money in the bank," we conclude.

"When we are older and things calm down," we say.

"When" never comes. When we arrive at our final destination, it is often too late. Many of us live life in fear of not reaching some magical destination, controlled by endless worry and denial of who we are and what we want today.

> Today, with small child in hand, let me dance!
> Today, with friend in hand, let me laugh!
> Today, with spouse in hand, let me love!
> Today, with me in mind, let me live!

THE DANISH TRAINS

I remember a great friend with whom I took a long train ride one day in October through the countryside of Denmark. Rene and I got along splendidly: I loved her wit and she valued my spontaneity.

Rene always knew life would eventually cheat her. She was convinced that she would be robbed of her greatest hopes. Young and naive, I assured her that her fears were unwarranted. I believed that life could not deny us from having a wonderful trip if we simply embraced the adventure. I failed to realize the powerful role self-esteem plays in determining how our lives turn out.

On our train ride we shared our hopes for future wedding nights with spouses yet unknown. Five years later I experienced mine. Twenty years later, having never married, Rene has yet to know if her wedding night fantasies will ever come true.

As the years passed, life confirmed her greatest fears. The worries that consumed her in adolescence became convincing obsessions as an adult. Rene clung desperately to our friendship over the years, becoming increasingly angry as my life worked and hers didn't. (Strange how two individuals can come to see life so differently over time.) Despite some painful life experiences—several dysfunctional relationships before I got married, suicidal thoughts following a near-fatal auto collision, and numerous other unpleasant "moments" in my life—I have come to more fully accept myself, others, and a loving God who wishes only the best for us. Rene, on the other hand, has written off God in her life.

"Ever since I gave up on God, I feel much better!" she told me. "I don't feel so vulnerable. I work the night shift at the U.S. Postal Service and take home a steady paycheck."

"You gave up God for the postal service? You must be kidding!" I said. (Considering my luck with the post office, I would have stuck with God.)

"Seems I always gave credit to God for the good things that happened in my life," she replied, "and I took credit for the bad. Somehow, I always got the rotten end of the deal. Now when I do good things, I give myself the credit!"

"And the bad you just blame on the post office!" I said.

"Well, I do have arthritis since I've been working there," she acknowledged, "but like I said, the pay is steady and the benefits are good. You know I need my security."

"Yeah," I remembered, "you always were concerned about making ends meet. You always thought you'd be the first to get the short end of the stick."

"And look what happened!" she said triumphantly. "I was unemployed for five years. I'm just grateful to have a job, regardless of the late hours and my arthritis."

"And you never had your wedding night," I reflected. "Do you ever think about your fantasy of how that night would be?"

"The best evidence I have that God is a man is the men I've dated!" she replied. "They have abandoned me the same way He did. I can't be bothered with any of them anymore. I like things just fine the way they are."

Rene was a victim of her fears; everything she feared for her future had come true. The later chapters in her book of life merely confirmed the earlier chapters I had witnessed firsthand. Her wedding night hopes were now just lost fantasies.

I loved Rene then. I love her today. And yet her story reads like a book I don't care to finish and would never recommend to a friend.

HOW DOES YOUR STORY LINE READ?

It is not what you get dealt in life, but your attitude toward life's challenges that determines how much you value yourself. People who like themselves will not be denied their happiness. They make time to live in the present. One of my favorite movie lines came from a character describing a thirty-five-year-old Yellow (*very* Yellow) bachelor. He worked as a part-time dance instructor for senior citizens.

"Jack," she said, "has failed at everything in life. Everything, that is, except living!"

What a remarkable epitaph for anyone. A quality life demands that we "seize the moments" and embrace the magic of today.

MY ACCOUNTANT

My business accountant, Dennis, is so fiscally responsible that he actually postponed his wedding until a year when his tax situation was better. Dennis constantly chides this Yellow client for not saving enough money for his retirement.

One day, I had heard enough and snapped: "Dennis, you spend your entire life worrying about how you can afford to live. I can't be forever bothered with your obsessions. Soon enough, we will both be old and feeble and our greatest thrill will be racing each other down the halls of the old folks home in wheelchairs. The only difference will be the abundance of memories colorfully etched in my mind of a lifetime filled with daily 'moments' of spontaneous adventures. You, on the other hand, will have money and a ledger to remind you exactly how much you spent!"

Yellows are not the only ones who live in the present. All colors are capable of discovering the magic of the moment. Mothers who swing with their children at the park rather than watch TV with them; fathers who coach the Little League teams to have fun, rather than just to win; friends who send birthday greetings or simply call to keep in touch with others' lives know the magic of valuing themselves.

People who take day hikes, spend an hour reading a book, or go barefoot long into the autumn know the power of valuing themselves. If you are finding reasons why you can't live for today, you simply don't value yourself. You are so busy burying yourself with rationalizations and justifications that you don't even realize you died. Wake up! Your life will only be a bad dream if you don't muster the courage to rewrite your story line before discovering your script has come to a tragic end.

People who value themselves, clean their house, dump the garbage, and renew their energy to live!

GET A LIFE

It has been said that the best defense is a good offense. The first line of a powerful offense in becoming charactered is developing, strengthening, and deepening your self-esteem. Valuing ourselves allows us to surrender our facades of fear and touch others' lives. A mysterious phenomenon happens when people learn to value themselves. Believing in themselves, they stretch beyond their comfort zones in order to more fully embrace others. They discover personal passions and pursue them. They experience life in the present, creating an exciting, multifaceted scrapbook of a well-lived life.

Valuing ourselves begins the charactering adventure. We must see ourselves as lovable and valuable simply because we breathe. As our story unfolds, we stretch to embrace all life offers. We learn to accept our limitations because they are easily offset by our innate and learned strengths. We exude the personal power we derive from discovering our passions and writing them into our daily scripts.

GOT A LIFE!

One day, Anne timidly entered my office. Attractive, overweight, and limited in a career far beneath her capabilities, she sought counseling because her children were ready to leave the nest and she wasn't ready to grant them wings. A Blue, Anne had been divorced for many years, and her entire life had been devoted to her children, with little regard for her own life. Recognizing that her life lacked purpose, she wanted to get a life but had no idea, short of getting pregnant again, how to do it.

We searched her childhood for dreams and fantasies of the life she hoped to live. I asked her to clip out any pictures or words that reflected a personal interest. She had always longed for a tropical vacation to Hawaii. However, the thought of actually being there was too great a leap. As is true of all psychological stretching, we must approach it one step at a time until we reach our goal. Anne took her first step by creating a lifestyle that included activities she enjoyed. She called friends for dinner, met men at dances, and traveled to neighboring San Francisco just for fun. In the summer, she spent a weekend with a girlfriend on the beach to get the feel of a Hawaiian vacation.

"I even wore shorts," she laughed, "which I wouldn't have been caught dead doing a year ago. You know how self-conscious I am about my weight!"

Anne was starting to come to life. With each step she risked more.

Small steps eventually became leaps until she called and informed me, "I'm booked for a week in Hawaii, and I just wanted to thank you in case I never come back."

She had come so far by simply embracing the gift of valuing herself. As author Sam Keen once said, "Our only security is our ability to change." Anne would agree.

People who value themselves engage in activities they value. Likewise, people who do what they enjoy value themselves. What do you enjoy? What feels good to you?

List ten activities you enjoy, anything that you feel is personally rewarding. These specific endeavors must come from within you. Do not write down what you, or others, think you "should" do. Be personal and specific, don't prioritize your answers; it's counterproductive at this point. Brainstorm with others or contemplate for yourself what makes you happy, or list activities you would like to try.

Ten Activities That Make Me Happy

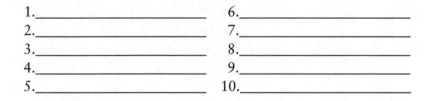

1._____   6._____
2._____   7._____
3._____   8._____
4._____   9._____
5._____   10._____

Now consider which activity brings you the greatest happiness, and why. In the chart below, rank them from the most valuable to least valuable. You will note that there are a series of boxes titled "variables" to the right of each listed activity. At the bottom of the boxes are symbols that reflect the variables for each activity. Place an X in any box that you answer in the affirmative. The symbols represent the following:

time: The last time you engaged in the listed activity.
phy: The activity requires physical exertion.
alone: You prefer to engage in this activity alone.
w/p: You prefer to engage in this activity with others.
new: You first experienced this activity this year.
tau: You have taught someone else to enjoy this activity.
$: This activity is relatively expensive.

Ten *Prioritized* Activities That Make Me Happy

	Activity	Variables						
1.								
2.								
3.								
4.								
5.								
6.								
7.								
8.								
9.								
10.								
		time	phy	alone	w/p	new	tau	$

Once you have completed this exercise, reflect on the insights you have gained about yourself and your preferred activities from your responses. Do you allow yourself much time to enjoy the activities you listed? How much have you valued yourself lately?

If you were accused of valuing yourself, would there be enough evidence to convict you?

Many years ago when I sat down and personally filled out my Ten Prioritized Activities That Make Me Happy list, I discovered how little I valued myself. True to my Yellow personality, I always found ways to have fun despite a heavy school load and work schedule while going to college. Married for several years, I had become consumed by my career and family responsibilities, so much that I forgot to value myself. I prioritized "being on the beach" as my number one activity and "playing tennis" as number two. When I reflected on the last time I actually went to the beach it had been over a year (I lived only twenty minutes away) and I couldn't remember the last time I had played tennis.

Seeing is believing. I had abandoned the two activities I enjoyed most in my life. Once I could clearly see how insensitive I had become to myself, I began spending lunch at the beach and evening hot dog roasts near the water. I was less successful with tennis. My wife already struggled with my long hours at work. Tennis would be yet another imposition on our family time. Over the next five years, I ignored my desire to play and let it simmer while I continued to work hard.

I was driving by the local tennis courts one day and decided to stop. I watched players making passing shots from the baseline that I used to make. I saw them pressing the other player and getting frustrated when their game didn't work. I enjoyed their efforts to execute new shots and their friendly rivalries, kidding each other about who was going to have to buy lunch after the match.

At that moment as I stood watching those tennis players on that tennis court, I realized I was cheating myself. I *liked* playing tennis.

That night when I walked into my house I announced to my wife, "Every Saturday morning for the rest of my life, I will be at the tennis courts. Don't try to stop me!"

She didn't skip a beat. "Good for you, honey," she said. "I think that's a great idea."

I was baffled at first. Then I was furious. "What do you mean, 'good for me and you think it's a great idea'?!" I demanded. "You are always the one with fifty reasons why I can't go."

"I know," she confessed. "I just never realized how much it meant to you. If it really means this much to you, I think you ought to go."

I will never forget that moment. How many years had I betrayed myself? All along I had been angry with her for preventing me from enjoying my life, when I should have been furious with myself. Now I was. You idiot, I thought. All these years you could have been playing tennis and you didn't take responsibility for yourself!

Valuing yourself is central to becoming a charactered individual. If you don't value yourself, your foundation for a quality life is always vulnerable. When we do not value ourselves, we can not fully value others. Valuing ourselves lets us stretch beyond our innate limitations to embrace the gifts the other colors bring at birth.

When we *value ourselves* we free a multitude of forces to come together to act on our behalf. Not only did I immediately sign up for tennis lessons and meet new friends who mutually enjoyed playing the game, but my wife also took lessons with me for a while. A few years later we moved to a new area complete with twelve tennis courts. Once I committed myself to enjoying the game, everything seemed to come together. I had affirmed myself and now life was affirming me.

LITTLE THINGS

Valuing yourself is best expressed in the little things of life. It isn't money or time that makes us happy; it is paying attention to the little things that brings happiness to our lives. It is the music you play that makes jobs such as cleaning more palatable. *It is the extra hour you spend with a friend at lunch or the midnight picnic you share with your children that puts your life on the map.*

Every day offers a new dragon to fight, and with time the daily battles of life lose their glamour. You may feel worn out in your efforts to keep up the good fight. Brighten your day and broaden your perspective with some personal truths; preferences that you enjoy simply because you breathe. Be accountable in choosing the activities that you value and discover the power that comes from loving the life you live and living the life you love. Simply stated, value yourself.

BINDING ATTITUDES AND BEHAVIORS OF EACH COLOR

The following lists illustrate reasons why each of the various personalities have difficulty valuing themselves. In becoming charactered, we must seek to identify how we sabotage our self-esteem. This requires humility to see ourselves accurately and courage to discover positive alternatives.

COMMON EXCUSES COLORS USE FOR NOT LEARNING TO VALUE THEMSELVES

REDS

1. I am only as good as my last project.
2. I am self-confident and that is the same as having self-esteem.
3. Expressing my feelings is not as important as getting the job done.
4. My worth is reflected by my success. I *am* what I *do*.
5. Fixing others gives me a strong sense of self-regard.
6. I get angry when others don't act as I know they should.
7. Life is too short for petty pleasure side trips.
8. Rescuing others is more comfortable than sharing with others.

BLUES

1. My self-esteem is based on high, unrealistic expectations.
2. My sense of worth is best experienced through others' success.
3. Gifts are less appreciated when they are not perfectly wrapped (symbolically).
4. My self-worth depends on the attitudes and behaviors of my family and close friends.
5. Self-doubt is proper modesty and reflects an honest appraisal of myself.
6. Work has greater value than play.
7. I deserve to be bitter considering what I have been through.
8. How can I enjoy today or think about the future when I haven't resolved my past?
9. How can I know whether I like myself when it could all change tomorrow?!
10. Seeing others happy is more enjoyable than taking care of myself.

WHITES

1. I like myself best when I'm alone.
2. Talking about my limitations doesn't help me learn to value myself.
3. Remaining unhappy is easier than confronting my fears.
4. I feel more comfortable not exposing my feelings and risking rejection.
5. I already accept myself just fine without complicated self-reflection.
6. If my happiness creates turmoil for another, I would rather simply go off and do what I want by myself.
7. Being at peace is more appealing than being happy.

YELLOWS

1. If I can't like myself as I am, it is too much trouble to change.
2. I expect instant gratification and even that takes too long.
3. Quality takes too much effort. Being less is good enough.
4. If you can't enjoy yourself, I can't be bothered with you.
5. Everyone tells me how likeable I am, so I must be.

Service is the optimum motive in becoming charactered. Service is best rendered by people who value themselves. It can be passed on to others only without strings, ulterior motives, force, or schedules. To serve others with this rare gift of valuing yourself is the highest form of art. It means accepting rather than expecting. Look at what activities make you happy. Like the butterfly, fly at your own pace and land where your heart rests secure.

If you discard the butterfly's method and force your way through life, always flying at others' pace (or demanding that they fly at yours), landing in relationships and jobs of insecurity and unrest, you will never master this essential step of charactered living. Don't fool yourself into thinking that you have learned to love yourself because of your accomplishments, when you have only learned to love what you can do. One day, you will discover that the world's applause cannot compensate for sincere self-fulfillment and valuing who you are.

SELF-ESTEEM IS CAUGHT, NOT TAUGHT

Self-esteem cannot be taught, but certain situations can be created which will give you a bigger catcher's mitt. You can create a scenario, a serendipity, whereby your opportunities to value yourself are substantially increased. Self-esteem can be role modeled, nurtured, and promoted. It must be chosen, not force-fed. It must be accepted and embraced by the recipient. The giver must be patient with their gift of self-esteem. Should the recipient choose not to receive the gift, it must remain with the giver.

It has always fascinated me how three children in the same family will often experience life through completely different eyes. For example, consider the busy career woman who volunteers as the local PTA president. With her hectic schedule, she is often gone from her three children at home. The children grow up, and reflecting back upon their childhood, each remembers Mom differently. One child is furious with his mother for rarely being home to cook dinner, and for never being around when he needed her. A second child loves all the excitement his mother's lifestyle brought to the home. He loved the interesting people who called and left messages for her. He enjoyed watching her dress up before going out for her meetings. And the third child never even remembers that she was gone, so what's to miss? Three children, three perspectives. Our childhood perspective depends on our childhood self-esteem. The facts don't change. The perspective does. We each create our own view of reality. Self-esteem brings brighter relationships and colors a more positive life.

CREATING SELF-ESTEEM

The best way to help children develop self-esteem is to create circumstances that enable them to 1) discover their preferences, and 2) develop the ability to make themselves happy. Role-model a happy life for them to see. It follows the axiom, "Catch a fish, feed a person for a day. Teach a person to fish, feed him for a lifetime."

Rather than depending upon others to make them happy, children discover the possibility of self-fulfillment. To develop self-esteem, a child must have the freedom to make her discovery, to create her own fishing expeditions.

Stanley Coopersmith documented this thinking with his renowned research study of 1,748 normal middle-school boys and their families over a six-year period. He states, "As a boy's parents see him, or as he thinks they see him, so he tends to see himself."

This powerful study provided numerous insights into providing a healthy home environment for the creation of self-esteem. The three significant findings of what enhanced a child's chances for choosing high self-esteem were:

1. *Love in the home.* This did not just mean hugging, kissing, and physical demonstrations, but specifically referenced a sincere respect and concern for the child.
2. *Accountability.* Parents of children with high self-esteem were significantly less permissive than parents of children with low self-esteem. Accountability played a critical role in developing self-esteem.
3. *A marked degree of democracy.* Families of children with high self-esteem established parents as fair leaders who were clearly "in change," yet also set a clear structure wherein children could make choices freely.

As expected, you will note that each of these three findings requires high self-esteem in parents as well. You simply can't provide effective environments for nourishing high self-esteem when you don't have it yourself.

SEIZE THE MOMENT

So many of us die long before we're buried. Life is filled with opportunities to value ourselves. This wonderful gift is free to any of us willing to "seize the moments" life offers. We must be careful not to focus too intensely on the future or be too regretful of the past. Valuing ourselves comes only in the present tense. It is in playing the game that we love ourselves. Reviewing trophies of past victories brings relatively little comfort. If you have children, hug them today. Wring the joy out of every moment just being with them, because tomorrow will be too late. We deceive ourselves into believing that there will always be another time. It is simply not so.

There are countless serendipitous attitudes and activities you can create in order to value yourself. Take the time to prioritize those activities that bring you a greater sense of yourself. This presents a problem for people who were deprived of play as children or who were ridiculed by peers or parents for being "different." You must first free yourself from biased negativity that taught you to withdraw and avoid honest self-expression. Find a role model and watch him or her live in the moment. Memorize his or her facial expressions and attitudes about people. Seek a mentor who can teach you how he or she learned to seize the moment and let tomorrow's fears take care of themselves.

When my wife and I were first married, she had no idea about the importance of play. I told her it was as vital to me as life itself. We always dated every weekend night and even some nights during the week, and she was amazed at the energy it created. Eventually, over time, she became a much more playful person. Now when I travel out of town on weekends, she is the one who tells me how boring it is staying home and how she misses our playtime. I became her role model and she actually mentored herself so that now she promotes living in the moment almost as much as I do.

What is perhaps most amazing about this story is the number of spouses out there who learned to criticize, whine to, or harp at their Yellow "embrace-the-moment" spouses, and never learned to enjoy their rich byproduct of valuing themselves because they only learned to do the things they were supposed to do rather than to do the things they loved to do.

If your life was so damaged as a child that you have no idea what you enjoy, go watch children, read a college catalogue, or pay attention to what catches your fancy. Try new activities, and don't be afraid to discard them if they prove unfulfilling. Remember that this is the gift Yellows bring to others. Yellows have no problem discarding activities and people they find boring. *The idea of not making everything sacred or necessary will free you to sample the activity or person rather than see it or him as a seven-course meal you are stuck with for life.*

CHAPTER FIVE

Step Two:
Seek Universal Truth

Universal truths are charactered individuals' laugh lines in life. To seek personal truths means to seek activities reflective of our individual style. However, to seek universal truths requires a lifetime of commitment to timeless concepts. Universal truths go beyond the limited boundaries of personality bias, and embody only consistent truths that always identify and predict human nature accurately, regardless of one's personality color or environmental custom.

King Arthur and his knights of the Round Table were well-known for their commitment to the charactered life. On one occasion, King Arthur queried of his great friend Merlin the Magician, "Which is the greatest quality of knighthood?"

"It is truth!" Merlin answered.

Truth! Even today his reply satisfies the basic requirement for becoming a charactered human being. While there are many universal truths with power to change the quality of our lives, I have only selected seven key universal truths which are essential to developing psycho-social-spiritual health.

UNIVERSAL TRUTH #1:
HUMILITY IS TO THE CHARACTERED SOUL
WHAT WATER IS TO THE BODY

Humility, like water, is our basic source of life. It opens our minds to new concepts and our hearts to new relationships. In fact, humility is such a critical universal truth that it was named as the first gift you must carry with you on your journey to become charactered. *Humility frees us from the rigidity that would deprive us from learning new insights and becoming charactered people.* Humility requires that we genuinely value ourselves as reflected by high self-esteem.

When depressed or arrogant people enter my office, I know I am in for a long battle to help them free themselves from their personal fears, self-abuse, and rigidity. Depressed people are in a dark hole and see no way out. Arrogant people are in the same dark hole but see no reason to get out. However, when ladders promising freedom are placed down their dark hole of limited perspective, they simply stare at their rescuer with jaundiced eyes of mistrust.

Both types of people remind me of the man who fell over a cliff and was miraculously saved from certain death when he grabbed a branch that had grown out from the rocks. Eventually his arms were in such pain that he knew he could not hold on much longer. In desperation, he called out to God.

"God, if You are there, help me," he yelled.

God responded, "I hear you, my son. Let go of the branch and you shall be free."

Now this was not what the desperate man had in mind.

"On second thought," he queried, "is there someone else up there I can talk to?"

Depressed people refuse to accept the answers to their problems, while arrogant people refuse to admit they don't already know the answers. However, neither the depressed nor arrogant person is willing to let anyone else help. Their minds and hearts are locked boxes to which only they hold the key, while secure people need no locks, freely inviting feedback from others. Insecurity breeds closed minds and hearts, locking others out of our lives. While arrogance and depression feel like different textures, they both produce the same tragic results.

Blinded by ourselves, we remain masked and unaware of how abundant our lives can be. Humility requires, and ironically creates, security.

Dr. Louis Aggaziz was a noted anthropologist who traveled all over the world, presenting fascinating lectures on his discoveries. One night following a presentation he gave in London, an older woman, quite depressed by her life, approached him and complained that life was unfair. "You travel all over and live like a king," she scoffed, "while I struggle just to survive."

"What is it you do for a living, madam?" he asked kindly, placing a ladder promising freedom down into her dark hole of limited perspective.

"I run an old folks home with my aging sister," she remarked, unaware of his magnanimous gift.

"What exactly do you do in the old folks home?" he pushed.

"I do *all* the cooking!" she exclaimed.

"Where do you spend most of your time when you do *all* the cooking?" he asked.

"If you really must know, I peel a lot of potatoes and sit on a stool by the sink." she retorted.

"What is under the stool?" he mused.

"Bricks!" she bristled. "Just bricks!"

Calmly, he proposed, "Write me a paper on the nature of bricks, if you will. I shall be happy to print your work and pay you for your efforts."

She determined to make him an honest man. She began her intensive study into the nature of bricks and eventually rendered him a rather expansive work on them. She submitted her completed document to Dr. Aggaziz, feeling rather smug for having beat him at his own game.

Upon receipt of her document, he circled the grammatical errors in the article, rendered payment, and wrote a brief note.

Dear Madam,

Your work is excellent. Please correct the minor grammatical errors and resubmit your article for publishing. Enclosed is the promised reimbursement for your trouble.

Sincerely,
Dr. Louis Aggaziz

P.S. What was under the bricks?

What was under the bricks? she thought. What an impudent man!

However, she had learned to trust Dr. Aggaziz's intentions and checked under the bricks. She discovered a research project of a lifetime, for under the bricks she discovered a vast community of ants.

ANTS!!! The answer was *Ants!* She dug even deeper into her study of ants than she had with bricks and eventually presented to Dr. Aggaziz an impressive literary work on the nature of ants. He published her work, and the financial rewards afforded her the opportunity to travel around the world.

Dr. Aggaziz was humble. He embraced this universal truth throughout his life, and anyone humble enough to hear his message discovered riches far beyond their initial imagination. His departing comments in life were, "There are no uninteresting things, only uninterested people."

Humility affords us opportunities to see our real selves for who we are and our real world which we create. Humble people find personal security within themselves. Humility frees us from our limitations and introduces us to the strengths the other colors have to offer. With humility we are able to turn our limitations and misfortune into strengths and success.

UNIVERSAL TRUTH #2:
ESTABLISH BOUNDARIES

Without question, the greatest contribution *The Color Code* makes is the understanding that each personality is driven by a unique motive. This insight offers tremendous power. To understand what drives each individual enables you to understand yourself and accept others. It is, however, even more important to know what drives your character. What treasures drive your life? What are your priorities? Where do you spend your time, and with whom? What annoys and delights you? What standards and ethics do you live by? And why?

Looking back at your life experience, it is often easier to see what you treasured. Hindsight brings a clearer picture of what your treasures have been and the things for which your heart has wished. Your most compelling thoughts and emotions eventually become expressed in your deeds.

Shannon was a delightful young teenager. Slight in build, she was almost waiflike in the company of her peers. She was pleasant, attractive, and well-liked. A popular baby-sitter throughout the neighborhood, Shannon's White personality was easy for both children and adults to be around. So easy, as a matter of fact, that no one ever noticed that Shannon's whole life was consumed with fear. One night, while baby-sitting our girls, she thought she heard a noise and quickly huddled with the girls in a dark corner of the living room, where no one could see in and they couldn't see out. The rest of the night they lay huddled together, too frightened to call her parents or the police for help. Shannon simply succumbed to her all-consuming fear.

Ten years later, Shannon had never married and held a menial job. She lived with her grandmother who protected her, and she risked nothing in creating or discovering a new life of her own. Fear still consumed this frightened young adult. She had no friends and she refused professional help. Shannon *treasured* fear and her heart still clung to false security. Note: Five years ago, Shannon woke up: She sought truth for the first time. She found professional help, began dating, and attends night school in pursuit of an exciting second career. Shannon's plight is further illustrated through the study of the dynamics of a young boy's life. Created for effect, his story is not real, but it imparts true concepts that explain the fear factor in many people's lives.

TRASH CAN LIDS

Stephen was a good boy. He caused few problems for his parents, which was a good thing, since their hectic lives were not programmed for distractions like children. Both held very responsible jobs and appreciated as little disturbance in the home as possible. However, much to their dismay, children *do* disturb.

One day Stephen's mother arrived home to discover her eight-year-old son crumpled in a ball on his bed. His face was bloody, and his torn shirt suggested that he had been in trouble.

"Stephen, what happened?" she screamed, reaching out to check more closely the scrapes and bruises on her son's face.

"Oh nothing," he whispered, hoping she would just let the question go unanswered. "Just a little problem on the way home from school. Do you think you could pick me up after my classes tomorrow?"

"You know your father and I work, Stephen," she said. "We can't pick you up from school every day. But I will take care of this problem. Tell me who did this to you and I'll call his parents."

Stephen would rather die than tell on the guys who did this. If his parents couldn't drive him home, he'd just have to figure something out on his own.

"Never mind, Mom. It won't happen again," he assured her.

She didn't believe him but thought, What's a working mother to do? I can't pick him up and he won't cooperate with names, so we'll just see what happens tomorrow.

The next day on his way home from school the older boys were waiting for him, snowballs in hand. Stephen ducked into an alley, desperately searching for something to defend himself. Suddenly a tomcat jumped from a trash can knocking the lid to the snow-covered cement. He picked up the trash can lid and raced by the older boys, shielding himself from their barrage of snowballs.

"Home free!" he shouted, once he arrived at his own home, closing the front door behind him. "Who needs my parents' help anyway? I've got all I need right here in my hand." With that, he triumphantly tossed the trash can lid onto his bed.

He shared his success with his parents over dinner. If Stephen was impressed, his parents were amazed.

"I just can't get over how wonderfully bright you are to have thought of defending yourself like you did," his mother gushed.

Throughout the rest of the winter, the boys with the snowballs persisted to attack him, but Stephen became even more adept with his trash can shield. His reputation spread through his entire school. The trash can lid became an obsession, replacing even his closest friends. It went wherever he went, because he suspected the older boys would always be waiting to seek their revenge.

Twelve years later, as a young man, Stephen met the girl of his dreams. Wedding plans were made and the day quickly approached for his bride to walk down the aisle. During the rehearsal, she approached the altar to find her future husband holding the trash can lid.

"What are you doing with that?" she asked.

"You know how many times it has protected me in my life, Jennie," he said. "Those older boys would love to get me on our wedding day."

"Have you completely lost your mind?" she demanded. "It's June. There is no snow outside."

"I know, but they could freeze ice. You have to understand how important this is to me."

"And you have to understand how important my wedding is to me!" she replied. "Either the trash can lid goes or I do!"

Stephen was confused. Why couldn't she understand how important this trash can lid had been? It had earned him the respect of his parents, friends, and most important, himself. If he had to choose between the trash can lid or Jennie, she would clearly have to be the one to go.

A ridiculous story? Well, the trash can lid is merely symbolic of so many things we embrace throughout our lives with equally tragic consequences. At the time, it appears that our hearts are focused on the right things for the right reasons, but we lose perspective. What was appropriate, even applauded at one time, is no longer legitimate. On the contrary, clean motives stand the test of time.

What are your trash can lids? Money? Alcohol? Religion? Anger? Trash can lids come in all shapes and sizes, and at various stages throughout our lives. Like Stephen, we pick up our trash can lids so subtly that we are often unaware of the serious consequences we must eventually pay for their embrace.

Everything we do in life has a price. Everything! To refuse to see our own heart's true intent is to remain oblivious to its destructive path. Somehow, we foolishly think that "we" are exempt from this universal truth. However, as overwhelming as it may seem, it is never too late to face your heart and honestly evaluate what it treasures.

Consider Marie, a strikingly attractive, if severe, woman in her fifties, whom I met by chance at a seminar she attended with her husband. When I shared Stephen's story about the trash can lid, Marie revealed the intense anger she felt toward her husband. Over their twenty years of marriage, Marie had learned to treasure petty victories of rejecting her husband before he could sarcastically reject her.

She chose "rejection" as her "trash can lid," and became a prisoner to her consuming anger and fear. For twenty years, she learned to hate herself for accepting life with her emotionally abusive spouse.

After the seminar, Marie searched her heart and reconsidered her "learned" treasures of resentment, anger, and stubborn resistance. She thought of how Stephen's trash can lid had eventually destroyed him and his relationship with his fiancée. One month later, I received this letter from Marie. While she writes from a comfortable distance, in the third person, her genuine sentiments reflect the sincerity and warmth of a charactered soul in the making.

Dear Taylor,

A man came one stormy night and talked of trash can lids. She was there, just a face in the crowd, entranced by his wit and charm, elevated by his insight and energy, as truth filled her ears. But then, not by choice, he came and revealed to her dismay a trash can lid, invisible to her eyes, hanging heavy round her neck. Like the soothing sound of falling waters, or the hush of rustling leaves in wind, he unloosed the cords that bound her to the old rusty lid.

She reached, to stop its falling, as it tumbled, crashing down around her feet. Shattered, broken in a thousand pieces, her heart began to weep. He only smiled, Leave it, and be free. Sobbing, deep moans rumbled through her soul, as she bent to gather up the pieces and take them as her own. She tenderly gathered and wrapped them in a cloth.

I'll carry this a little longer. Without it I am lost, she thought. She traveled to a hillside, and sat her bundle down. Naked now in sunlight, exposed to its rays, she turned and walked away. But her sobbing would not cease, for the thing she left behind, buried in the side of the hill, had protected her from life.

It was black and dirty, dented from much use. It had shut out light with its thick and filthy iron crust. Still, it was her companion—one that she could trust. As she walked, now empty-handed, vulnerable to sun and rain, she bowed her head and prayed . . .

A warm and gentle feeling softly filtered through her soul, drenching every corner of her lonely darkened form. The man had gone as quickly as he came. Yet he had unloosened her soul, and invited her to live again. How can I thank you for making such an impact on my life. I love you and thank you for freeing me of my trash can lid in life.

Marie

Six months later Marie and her husband attended one of my retreats in Sundance, Utah, where I personally witnessed Marie's transformation. She was, once again, in love with her husband and her life. No longer severe in appearance, she displayed compassion for her husband, touching his arm throughout the retreat; something she had not done in over twenty years. Her "treasures" were new and her heart was very much alive.

What are your treasures? Who has your heart? We get what we deserve from life. We create our relationships, our trash can lids, our consequences. Admit the truths of your heart. Become accountable for the treasures you pursue. Personal power comes from knowing what we treasure and *why* we treasure it.

UNIVERSAL TRUTH #3:
PERSONAL POWER IS THE FOUNDATION
FOR CHARACTERED LIVING

"She just slammed her bedroom door in my face and flipped me off!" Susan shouted. "Now how am I supposed to handle that kind of treatment from my fifteen-year-old daughter? She was out until two A.M. and she knows perfectly well that her curfew is midnight. She smells like a strong blend of liquor and vomit, and still expects me to believe that she was late because her boyfriend locked his keys in the car. That's the oldest line in the book. Then she comes in the house and goes straight to her room and gets completely under her covers. So I tell her she is grounded for life and threaten to rip up her paycheck from work if she doesn't come out from under the covers and talk to me this very minute. She flips me off again but refuses to show me her face buried under the covers. I want to rip her head off but I'll go to jail, so I rip up her paycheck instead. Finally I realize that I am totally out of control so I go to my own bedroom furious with her as well as myself. I can't sleep until four-thirty A.M. I just keep thinking that I have to get a grip on things. I realize that I am completely out of control with this girl."

Susan is honest, candid, and endearing—one of my favorite people in the world. She is also out of control. She has no personal power and her daughter knows it. In fact, she counts on it.

89

Right now every teenager in America wants Susan to be their mother. Who could pass up such a deal? Free room and board, and no one able to tell them what to do. Susan would be a hot ticket on the "pick-a-parent" parade!

Personal power is the foundation for charactered living. Personal power requires that you value yourself. Positive self-regard enables you to establish certain boundaries for others to behave within when they interact with you. It clearly delineates what you will and won't accept from them. Personal power establishes your limits.

Susan's lack of personal power creates vague boundaries and confusing limits for her daughter *and* herself. Susan is simply a lot of bark. Personal power adds "bite" to your "bark." Commit yourself to your values. If *you* can't, how can you expect others to?! The Susans of the world often allow (even breed) dysfunctional relationships because they lack a consistent commitment to themselves and their core values in life.

Personal power must come from within yourself. It's how you carry yourself. It's how you handle (or avoid) conflict. It's how you accept (or reject) criticism. Like the math equation $2 + 2 = 4$, personal power is a universal truth that consistently sets positive boundaries for your interpersonal relationships.

Personal power defines what attitudes and behaviors you will accept, and what the consequences are for anyone who crosses the line. People with personal power know their rights and appropriately assert them.

Personal power requires being one hundred percent responsible for yourself and what happens in your life. Blaming others only sabotages this principle of character building. Unaccountable people prolong their role as victims. Victims often victimize others who suffer from limited personal power as well. *Water seeks its own level, and people seek relationships equal, and deserving, of themselves.*

POWERLESS VICTIMS

Lisa and John deserved each other in their respective victim roles of a pathological Blue and dumb Red. John was brilliantly successful in his business career and terribly inadequate at home. Lisa refused to take responsibility for her empty life, and raced from psychotherapist to priest, spreading her unhappiness, hoping to find a sympathetic ear, while simultaneously pursuing a seven-year affair because she felt "emotionally deprived" by John.

Both demonstrated a strong dependence on each other. Neither planned to change (typical of insecure victims), but both blatantly attacked the other's inadequacies throughout their relationship. One role that I refuse to play as a psychotherapist is the referee. It's a lot like professional wrestling. There may be legitimate pain inflicted, but in the end the results are stilled rigged and the referee merely becomes part of the scam, guilty by association.

"Why are you still together?" I once asked, realizing that they deserved each other and lacked the personal power necessary to create new lives for themselves.

John volunteered that he was staying in the marriage because he didn't think it would be good for the children if she reared them alone. Lisa explained that she stayed because she wasn't strong, enough to be on her own. Neither would set legitimate boundaries for their relationship. After several months, I requested that at least one of them develop the personal power to make a decision that would move their stagnant relationship off dead center. They chose, instead, to flee my office and professional intervention. Neither was capable or willing to face life without the other. Yet both reserved the rights to their misery and endless complaints about being stuck with each other for life.

Psychotherapists, as agents of change, are often granted excellent seats to observe people transcend personal inadequacy and embrace personal power in their lives. It is quite the amazing miracle. While most people prefer comfort zones and status quos, there are those rare charactered individuals who refuse to be denied a quality life. Changing oneself necessarily changes others in the relationship. Since others aren't usually requesting a change simultaneously, they can be brutal toward the one who changes the pattern of the relationship without their consent. Fortunately, when individuals have their personal power intact, they are less concerned with others' approval for charactered change. They simply redesign the dysfunctional aspects in their relationships by establishing new boundaries and walking a higher path.

Personal inadequacy renders us vulnerable to a myriad of wasted relationships and time-consuming activities. Personal power frees us to be productive and pursue energizing opportunities. It enables us to eliminate limited entanglements and/or negative commitments while breeding self-confidence and self-respect.

MARIJUANA BROWNIES

Our church youth group once designed an activity to teach the importance of developing personal power and making proper choices in life. An entire gymnasium was decorated to represent a variety of life experiences. Some were beneficial; others were not. Positive booths promoted life-affirming activities such as building friendships, getting an education, and physical fitness. Booths promoting negative life experiences espoused quick fixes and cheap thrills. My booth sold drugs, enticing the youth with delicious fake marijuana brownies, baked to perfection.

Each participant was given play money and told to spend their money wisely at the booths displaying various life experiences. At an unknown time a bell would ring and they would be asked to give an accounting of how they spent their money "in life." Booth owners were instructed to convince the young participants to spend their money at their booths. The activity began and the kids raced toward the booths offering quality life experiences.

For twenty minutes I sat idly with my fake marijuana brownies while the young people smugly passed by, refusing to spend even a dime on drugs, which they knew would bring them little respect at the end of the activity. Instead, they crowded into the booths promoting higher education, service, and physical fitness. No one was willing to part with their money for my brownies.

Then I remembered how drug dealers promoted their merchandise on the streets. I enticed young "dealers" with a cut of the action: I would pay them so they wouldn't have to spend a dime of their own money to get "high." The appeal of something for nothing was contagious and suddenly I was rolling in business. I picked up twenty "dealers" in ten minutes.

"Sounds like fun," one kid said. "Let's get Freddie and Cheryl. They still have some bucks."

The word spread like wildfire. Soon I had over fifty young people selling brownies just for the thrill of it. We were in mass production while many of the positive "life experience" booths were now empty. Some of the adult leaders became concerned and demanded that I be shut down. The chairman refused.

"This is an opportunity for our youth to make their choices and spend their money and time as they wish," he explained. "It is not our place to intervene yet. If there are prices to be paid, they must wait until the activity ends."

Drug dealing became so successful that I created a pyramid and paid my top dealers a greater cut from the profits they earned. They were envied by the other kids and ecstatic with their drug-dealing success. More than one hundred kids wanted a piece of the action before time was called and the activity came to a close.

"Time's up!" the leader signaled by ringing a loud bell. "Everyone find the booth that consumed most of their time and sit near it."

Over half of the kids circled my drug booth. Still buzzing from the excitement of it all, they laughed and bragged and swapped stories of their successes.

"The activity has come to an end." the leader said. "Whatever money you have left is worthless. The only things of value in your 'life experience' have been earned at the booths of friendship, literacy, family, physical fitness, service, education, and mental health. If you have four or more tokens from these booths, you have lived a quality life. If not, consider yourself a failure."

If I live to be one hundred years old, I will never forget the expressions on the faces of the young people at my booth. Their faces were etched in despair. Many were furious with me, as though I had betrayed them. It wasn't the money, however, I had robbed them of. It was their time and energy. I had drained them of all their time and given them a false sense of security with their focus on dealing drugs. At "life's end," they were left empty and had no one to blame but themselves. Like John and Lisa, rather than developing personal power, they trapped themselves with other victims and headed down a dead-end path.

Personal power refuses to transfer blame and responsibility to others. It remains completely within yourself. When we blame others for our plight in life, we fail to realize that if someone else holds the keys to solving our problems, we are powerless to become healthy unless and until *they* change. Without personal power, we remain victims to a life controlled by someone else. Like John and Lisa or the "drug-dealing youth," we have no one to blame but ourselves.

Personal power comes from valuing ourselves and understanding universal truths. Charactered people set acceptable attitude and behavior boundaries for all with whom they interact. They are comfortable with their rights and insist on proper limits in communication. Personal power frees us to eventually develop successful relationships through the optimum motive of serving others.

UNIVERSAL TRUTH #4:
FREE AGENCY IS THE CORNERSTONE
OF THE HUMAN EXPERIENCE

> *If you love someone, set them free;*
> *if they come back, they're yours;*
> *if not, they never were.*

Of course, angry Blues think it should read: "If you love someone, set them free; if they come back, they're yours; if not, *hunt them down and kill them.*"

Free agency is a close relative of clean motives. Granting free agency to others may feel like you are walking a tightrope without a safety net. However, with clean motives, you are actually on very safe ground. When I free you to choose your path, I am saying I trust you, and myself, to accept the consequences of your choices. We cannot predict the future with free agency. We simply accept the fate of others' decisions as they come. "Letting go" places a mirror before us, forcing us to face our inability to control others.

Granting other people free agency places the same mirror of accountability before them, requiring that they eventually be accountable for their "free" decisions. They face both their right to make choices, as well as the accountability for the choices they make. Fortunately, our mirror is double-sided. The mirror of free agency exposes our strengths as well as our limitations. To become charactered requires freedom in order to know what really motivates us and how we would truly choose to act, given the opportunity. For example, we cannot know if a prisoner is rehabilitated until he is freed from his locked cell. We cannot know even our children's fate until we free them to pursue a life on their own.

Jason moved from a comfortable life in Southern California to the rugged mountains of Maine in a conscious effort to keep his wife and children from his childhood, of which he was deeply resentful. His father was a successful attorney and bewildered by his son's choice to abandon the "enviable" lifestyle he had worked so diligently to provide. Jason's father learned too late that you cannot force a child to accept a lifestyle you impose on him.

Jason hated his father's alcoholism, his pompous Red arrogance, and his rigidity. He pitied his mother's feeble attempts to challenge his overbearing father. He always knew, once free, he would choose a life quite different from the one he became familiar with as a child.

Jason is not alone. We all must accept responsibility for our choices in life. As with both Jason and his alcoholic father, we are all ultimately free to choose our path in life and must, therefore, be accountable for the path we choose.

Insecure people are generally consumed with everyone else's paths *NB* rather than accepting responsibility for the one they walk. Ironically, insecure people feel so out of control personally, that they often expend tremendous energy seeking to control others. Fishermen tell me that if two lobsters are placed in the same cage, neither will escape. When one tries to climb out, the other one pulls it back to the bottom. Both remain imprisoned by each other's fears. Insecure people spend tremendous energy sabotaging others in life, pulling them down so as not to be left alone at the bottom of their "caged" existence. Insecurity breeds insecurity. The gift of free agency is literally every individual's ticket out of victimized bondage.

Charactered people choose carefully how they spend their energy in life. They control others only when it is in both people's best interest. They choose to exercise their free will only in order to enhance the quality of their life, rather than simply making a statement. Freeing oneself to experience life more abundantly requires tremendous self-discipline and self-acceptance. Once we accept ourselves, we free ourselves to love *and* to be loved.

Carol was like a soft breeze on a warm day—quiet, subtle, and inviting. I liked her the minute I saw her. She traveled more than six hours in a car with four small children to meet with me, and as I listened to her story, I remember candidly thanking God for bringing her into my life.

Her mother was a diagnosed bi-polar schizophrenic, who spent eleven out of twelve months each year in a mental hospital. She died when Carol was twelve years old. Carol continued doing what she had always done—fixing meals, washing clothes, and helping her siblings with homework. Her father was an alcoholic and heavily involved in pornography. Her three brothers followed in their father's footsteps, abusing alcohol and pornography, while Carol chose the charactered path. She used her free agency to invite positive role models into her life. She spent a lot of time with a family who lived down the street.

"The mother of this family was a remarkable woman," Carol said gently. "I would just drop by and spend hours with her. She was always nice to me. I would come over to her house and sit on the couch in the living room and play with her children, help with dinner, or just talk. I simply enjoyed being around her and she always made me feel good about myself."

"So she understood your difficult circumstances at home and offered to intervene?" I asked.

"Actually, she had no idea what was going on in my home, and as a White, I never considered it my place to tell her," Carol said. "Years later, after I graduated from college, I went back to my hometown and visited her. Something came up in our conversation about my father and his recent problems with the law. This woman gasped when I told her that his problems with drinking and sex had been going on for years. I couldn't believe she didn't know.

" 'What must you have been thinking all those years when I came to your home just to be with you and your family?' " I had asked the woman. " 'You even let me live with you for a week sometimes. And now I discover that you didn't even know why I was there?' "

By now, the woman was in tears. She took Carol in her arms and hugged her, as she had often done when Carol was a child, and said, "Carol, I am so sorry. I had no idea that your home life was so unhappy. I knew that your mother had serious mental problems and your dad drank a lot but never considered the amount of abuse you had suffered. I simply enjoyed having you around."

Both Carol and this woman had mastered the art of using free agency wisely in creating healthy relationships. The optimum motive of service requires that we exercise our free agency wisely, as reflected in the lives of both women. Carol's three brothers exercised their free agency as well. They simply chose not to stretch beyond their "caged" existence and made unwise decisions.

Carol and her brothers are not alone. Daily, we use our free agency in choosing to accept or reject the charactered path.

UNIVERSAL TRUTH #5:
WHAT GOES AROUND
COMES AROUND

What goes around really does come around. With age and experience, I have witnessed the validity of this universal truth. You can run, but you cannot hide. However you live, you will be rewarded.

Gladys is a charactered sixty-year-old Red woman who cares for her handicapped husband in California and both of her aging parents, who live in Detroit. Recently she sought my advice in sorting out the details of her upcoming visit to Detroit to handle her aging parents' affairs.

"My mother was recently placed in a rest home," she explained. "She told me over the phone that she has no intentions of ever going home to live with my father again. She has had it with my father's endless complaining and miserable attitude. Mom will be fine because she has created friendships throughout her life with a nurturing sincerity that benefits everyone lucky enough to know her. She has friends of all ages because of her compassion and the service she has rendered through the years."

"The problem," Gladys continued, "is my father. He doesn't know that she is not coming home. He is such a poor excuse for a human being and always has been. He berates everyone. No one, including my brother and I, respect him or want to be around him. Unfortunately, my father has never cast his bread upon the water. There is nothing out there to come back in his hour of need. It is so difficult to believe that anyone could be so empty, but quite frankly, he is only getting what he deserves. It just seems like a huge price to be paying all at once. They say what goes around comes around, and his is coming around in spades!"

A SIMPLE PHRASE

A great king called all his wise men throughout the kingdom and requested that they determine the most important truth he should live by in life. The wise men studied and debated for days before coming to agreement on the following advice.

"Your Honor," they said, after much research, "we must tell you that the greatest truth you should live by comes in a simple phrase."

"Well, what is it?" he impatiently demanded.

"There is no free lunch," they said.

At first, the king was greatly displeased. He thought they were making a mockery of his request. With time, however, he discovered the power in these few words of wisdom.

When we only put in half a day's work, we are only half a person. We often think we are kidding others when we get away with only giving half efforts, but we are truly kidding ourselves. Ralph Waldo Emerson once shared, "Everything has a price." In this example, the price would be self-respect and integrity. In Gladys's father's life, the price is loneliness and despair.

Consider our environment: Today we are paying dearly for our ignorance and environmental abuse of the past. Prices are often deferred so that future generations must help clear the debt left by previous villains. Consider the plight of children with alcoholic parents who must learn to trust as adults because they were deprived of that right as children. They must pay the price for their dysfunctional childhoods, or remain victims of distrust and abusive cycles for life.

At numerous places on the charactered individual's path, one must pay his dues. The farther we journey without covering our debts, the greater the price will be. We can not escape justice. When we search our lives and admit our dysfunctions and/or dirty motives on a regular basis, we feel humble and our personal power is increased. "Coming clean" is one of life's most freeing experiences. We must not let fear convince us that "just this once" our lunch is free. There is always a price and charactered people pay their debts.

BRAD

One of my most rewarding therapeutic interventions came in disguise. Brad was a bright young man with a refreshing optimism and quick wit. Disabled from a medical malpractice, this thirty-year-old single man refused to let his physical pain keep him down. He was intense with his feelings and deliberate in his actions. It quickly became evident that Brad wanted help with a much more serious matter.

"I know you know why I have come to see you," he asserted after seeing me about a month. "You already have it figured out, don't you? I want to tell you and that is why I keep coming back. I need desperately to trust someone," he said, looking away from me. "I hope you are the right one to tell. I have had so much bottled up inside me for so many years."

Brad had never shared his frustration with his homosexual identity, which he had struggled with for decades. Over the next eight months we processed all the feelings, emotions, and behaviors he had experienced in his dual life. Such an intense Blue individual does not superficially experience anything—especially a sexual identity.

After years of empty sexual activity and tired of living alone, he decided he wanted to share his life with someone. He wished it could be a woman but felt it must be a man. He pursued and found a man. Before engaging in a full-fledged sexual relationship, however, they both agreed to be tested for HIV. Brad tested positive. Neither expected the test results. Both agreed to terminate the relationship.

"Now I must pay the price," he said, weeping.

Now he would pay for the "free" lunches in his life. Now he would clear his debt. He was a devastated human being.

Initially, he experienced tremendous anger at God and himself for "being the way he was." Then he attacked his father for not loving him enough. Eventually he blamed almost everyone. Exhausted, he finally surrendered, and accepted a more charactered path. He began lifting weights regularly, taking medication, and dating women. He knew he needed to find a woman who could accept him with the complete knowledge of his sexual identity issues and the disease that now consumed him. He rejected the homosexual lifestyle because he felt he could no longer live in a world that had infected him with cause for a premature death.

He found Beverly. Beverly had her own sexual dysfunction and frustration with men. She was neurotic in relationships and skillfully dodged men for thirty-one years. Marriage to a handsome, caring (albeit homosexual) man appeared to be a stroke of luck to Beverly. Neither cared much for a sexual relationship with the other, which sealed the deal.

Three weeks following their wedding, Brad entered my office completely frustrated, "If I had known any human being could be this inadequate, I would have never married her," he said. "She is a slob, completely inconsiderate, and emotionally retarded. I thought I would have to go to the bottom of the barrel to find someone who would have me in marriage, and I obviously did."

Prices! We must pay for our lunch. He could not expect to find a quality woman when he was not willing to be a quality man. He claimed that he simply could not give to a woman what he felt for men. He did not love and cherish this woman. He did not adore her. He simply married her because it seemed like an appropriate thing to do before he died. He refused to live a homosexual lifestyle because he thought it had turned on him. Yet, he was equally resolved not to turn toward her.

Brad was finished with his lunch and standing at the cash register of life. It was time to pay the price. However, the cashier offered him a way to pay for his meal. Brad was encouraged to serve his spouse. Regardless of his reason for marrying her, he was capable of loving her, if only as another human being. Leaving the cash register, Brad discovered the power in service.

He reflected on how he had learned to accept his HIV status and renewed his will to live. He decided the same could be true with his marriage. Brad forgave himself and Beverly for all of their limitations and felt an increase of love for himself and his wife. He began appreciating unique ways that she blessed his life and expressed his appreciation daily. He nurtured her self-esteem. He served her without expectation. Still misunderstood for his sexual preference, he chose to understand his wife and her needs. He sought to serve, rather than be served.

Today they enjoy a marriage of limited, though creative sexuality.

More important, they have created an enviable love; love that will endure what many heterosexual couples don't know. Brad pursued the charactered path. He decided to pay his dues and enjoy his expensive, albeit paid-for, lunch.

MATT

Matt's search for universal truth came in a similar package but with different wrapping. Matt was married and had a ten-year-old daughter who was the light of his life. While Brad had been self-obsessed with his sexual needs and personal vanity, Matt was still a child in his forty-year-old body. He surfed every day before going to work and slammed cupboards when life didn't agree with him. However, his business mask controlled his life. He borrowed money extensively from his successful parents, promising someday to repay his growing debt, but knowing someday would never come. His life was filled with free lunches.

Reflecting on his father's loving involvement with him as a young man, Matt shared how his dad had always listened and stood by him. His dad was as involved in Matt's life as Matt allowed him to be. When he saw Matt make poor choices, he reminded him that life was cyclical—a continuous circular motion. He assured Matt that no matter how far he went away, he was on the very same path that will bring him closer to his mother and father later in life.

"I married a pathological Blue woman with tremendous mood swings. She resents my nature—my whole lifestyle for that matter. Through the years I have watched our marriage deteriorate, and decided that I made my bed and deserved to lie in it. However, when I saw my wife verbally beat up my daughter, I knew the bed had become too hard. My parents suggested seeing you, and they haven't been wrong yet, so here I am."

"First, we must get you clean," I told him. "You have to learn to value yourself and role-model a lifestyle your daughter will want to embrace. Perhaps even your wife will find you more appealing. To love the unlovable, you must first love yourself. Let's focus on those activities you value. Before we can help your family, we have to find you."

"What do you mean, 'find me'?" he asked. "I think I make sense. My life works. I just can't let my wife abuse my daughter."

"What you can't let happen," I said, "is what you are doing to yourself. Matt, we are born with innate personalities complete with motives that drive us. To find you, we must know you. To know you requires knowing what motivates you. We must understand your innate strengths and limitations."

Matt's first major breakthrough came during a hypnotic regression to his childhood. He discovered himself as a child playing on the beach. He spent the afternoon revisiting his home and friends. He embraced himself as a child to say good-bye and a wave of emotion swept through him like a tornado. Through the years, Matt had grown distant from himself. He had abandoned his personality and true identity. Revisiting himself as a child gave him the confidence to center himself again. We discovered Matt was actually a Yellow who had learned to wear the mask of a Red.

Matt had betrayed himself by abandoning his innate personality for a learned personality unnatural to him and which was guaranteed to sabotage his potential for living a charactered life. He disliked himself and rejected his core motive, instead of embracing his father's personality which he admired and trusted. He pretended to live his life as though he were his Red father, hoping to experience his father's success. However, his gifts were not his father's gifts and his motives for discarding his innate personality were dirty. He married poorly because he didn't know himself and handled business poorly because he was pretending to be someone he wasn't.

With therapy, he agreed to go home; not to his parents, but to himself. Home to the Yellow child he had cast aside. Home to the sensitive soul who loved people; the trusting optimist without guile. He did not have to abandon the wonderful Red gifts he had learned in life. He only needed to put them in perspective.

As expected, his decision to grow up and face himself threatened his wife and their questionable marriage. She rebuffed his efforts to change. *The weakest link always controls the relationship.* She could see only her pain and made his life difficult, but Matt knew his life must be different and refused to run back to his previous life of facades. He stretched emotionally, mentally, and spiritually. In time, her emotional abuse no longer found fertile soil in his heart and her verbal attacks simply became wasted rhetoric. He had found his true self and his discovery had strengthened his resolve to be whole. Matt was standing at the cash register of life and was prepared to pay for his lunch.

UNIVERSAL TRUTH #6:
AFFIRMATIONS BRING RESULTS

Beth was an engaging woman in her early fifties who looked like she wasn't a day over forty because she kept herself in terrific physical shape playing tennis and doing aerobics. Beth's motto was "Go for it" and she enjoyed a multifaceted life. She traveled often and has enjoyed tremendous success in her career as a school principal.

What Beth wanted most in life was a loving relationship with a man. What Beth wanted second most in life was a Mercedes. I met her one year before she got her Mercedes.

She drove into the school parking lot at her office and honked her new horn until the entire staff could no longer ignore her.

"Rather impressive!" I shouted. "You always said you would be driving a Mercedes one day and look at you now. You really know how to treat yourself right."

She looked like a child at Christmas. It was exactly as she had envisioned it to be. More than a car, however, her Mercedes was a reality, envisioned many years earlier in the form of a dream.

"People really don't know how long I have lived for this moment," she explained. "I have known I would be driving this car for five years and today I feel like I'm on fire!"

Beth built her fire many years ago and nurtured it from small kindling until it could burn brightly on its own. She had consistently worked for five years to make this dream a legitimate reality. Beth attended a seminar on affirmations five years ago. The seminar leader challenged her to get a clear vision of what she wanted her life to be and how committed she was to making the necessary changes. She randomly listed each affirmation on a sheet of paper and subsequently prioritized them. Second on her list was the Mercedes.

"I really don't know why having a Mercedes was so important to me, but it always has been," Beth said. "Even as a young girl, I remember thinking that I wanted to drive one. When I made my list, it was clearly number one. It was not difficult for me to get behind this affirmation and believe that it would someday be a reality."

Every day she pulled out her list of top five affirmations and reviewed them. She carefully visualized in her mind how each of them would make her feel when she actually achieved them. She placed another list of the same five affirmations on her bathroom mirror and read them twice a day. She believed she deserved to drive the Mercedes and committed to a lifestyle that would facilitate her success.

However, Beth's real number one priority was to establish a loving relationship with a man. Subconsciously frightened that it could never be a reality, she refused to place it on her list of affirmations.

Her first marriage to an alcoholic ended in divorce, and Beth maintained a wonderful relationship with her children. She met her grown daughters weekly for lunch. She was competitive, athletic, responsible, and compassionate. She embodied so many attractive characteristics that it puzzled many as to why she was unable to piece together a quality relationship with a man.

Careful scrutiny of Beth's unresolved childhood made it painfully clear why she had been unable to do so. Her father was an alcoholic and she had never dealt with the emotional scars of her father's abusive lifestyle. She repeatedly attracted men who were incapable of sharing the quality of life she envisioned for herself.

Lacking self-esteem in personal relationships, Beth pursued unhealthy relationships she would never have allowed to exist in her professional life. Beth was clear about her professional expertise, but vague and confused about her rights in personal relationships. She would meander through men without a clue as to what she was doing. She always found new relationships but having never resolved her jaded perceptions of men, she continually dug up poor material to work with. Nonetheless, she pressed on. Each relationship loss would break off another piece of her heart and her self-confidence until she was sure she would never have a quality relationship with a man.

What was the difference in her ability to affirm driving a Mercedes and her inability to affirm having a loving relationship with a man? Some would say Mercedes are simply more reliable. Perhaps. (Actually, men do quite well with regular tune-ups.) The truth is simply a matter of "getting what you see." Beth never really *believed* she would have a quality relationship with a man. She never "saw" it happen. Unresolved anger at her father and disgust for his destructive lifestyle diverted her energies toward a professional career and living life on her terms. Her vision and her heart won the Mercedes. She never got past first base affirming a quality relationship with men because she never believed or could honestly see it happen.

Beth is a perfect example of why affirmations succeed and fail. She believed in her right to own a Mercedes. She also believed she did not deserve to have a quality relationship with a man. Affirmations begin where you believe. It is not just a matter of describing your wishes. Affirmations are concrete realities in the making. Whatever you truly believe will be yours, will be. Good or bad, the results will be the same. It is an absolute universal truth of mental health.

Ask yourself what you believe in. What personal life patterns expose your true beliefs. Brainstorm all the things you want in life. Write down everything in a random fashion. Go back and delete those things that are mere wishes and not capable of stirring your passions enough to make them a reality. Take each of the remaining possibilities and consider whether you really believe you deserve to have them in your life.

Check your motives. Are they clean? Ask why you want this affirmation in your life. Consider how you will feel when you have achieved each of the affirmations. How will each affirmation color your life? Prioritize each of the affirmations from most important to least important. Limit your list to the top five affirmations. Seek role models who have successfully affirmed gifts you want in your life. Begin spinning your dreams into realities.

The exact number of affirmations is unimportant. However, it is important to limit them to a manageable number in order to feel confident that you can accomplish them. Unmanageable affirmations become unrealistic wish lists that you eventually toss. Affirmations take time to realize. By the time you weave five affirmations into realities, old considerations may have lost their appeal. Begin anew the entire process by creating new affirmations. Ironically, many people who experience success with affirmations forget to renew the process.

One man explained that he had always longed to live by the ocean. He created this affirmation and began weaving his dream into reality. He truly believed he deserved and wanted this to be a part of his life.

"I not only succeeded in creating this wonderful reality, but I even surprised myself at how quickly it happened," he said. "That was over five years ago and I have not developed one single affirmation since. To be quite honest, I am embarrassed to admit it."

It is puzzling why people forget to exercise a process that once worked so well. However, it is not uncommon to hear success stories from individuals who applied the principle, enjoyed the reward, and subsequently let this universal truth slide. Becoming charactered asks that you affirm your life while surviving life merely requires that you roll with the punches. The charactered path requires that you dictate the level of play and believe that you deserve to win. Today is a good day to dream.

UNIVERSAL TRUTH #7:
CHARACTERED INDIVIDUALS
ARE BEST REMEMBERED FOR THE GIFTS
THEY STRETCH TO GIVE

While healthy people are appreciated for giving the gifts of their innate personality, charactered lives are best remembered for the gifts they stretched to adopt from their innate colors. We place a greater value on their "acquired gifts" because of the tremendous effort they must exude in order to earn the gift prior to sharing it with others.

The optimum motive for the charactered life is to serve. To serve others requires genuine respect for universal truth. We must seek to understand people through their eyes and serve them in their color. To overcome the discomfort of speaking in another's native tongue, we must value ourselves and those with whom we speak. To do so requires a willingness to fail. We can not know how to speak another's language without practice. We will make mistakes. Learning to walk, we fall many times before establishing ourselves comfortably as "walkers." However, life's greatest joys are found beyond the limited gifts we bring with us from birth. To discover life's highest meaning, we must keep trying; keep getting up; keep asking for humility to understand, courage to risk, and grace to endure the charactered path.

CHAPTER SIX

Step Three:
Clean Your Motives

It is only with the heart that one can see rightly.
—*The Little Prince*

Truth can be so annoying! Both my personal life and my professional
career have taken me places I would have rather not been and forced
me to face realities I would have rather not faced. I have wrestled with
the demons within myself as well as those embodied in others. Not all
battles have resulted in wins. They have not all been losses either.
Somewhere along the charactered path, however, I have learned that
win or lose, the entire game of living is weighed in the balance of one's
motives.

It is not the money we make or don't make. It is not the number of
children we rear or refuse to give birth to. It has nothing to do with
the occupation we choose or clothes we wear. The charactered life is
determined by *why* we do what we do.

Ultimately, the motive behind our thoughts and behaviors determines whether our lives have been successful.

Motives are our reasons that cause us to think and behave as we do.
Motives are either clean or dirty. There is no gray area in between.
Clean motives benefit everyone. Dirty motives are always biased on
one party's behalf. Most of us rarely seek the real reasons for our attitudes and behaviors, preferring to rationalize, justify, or simply deny
why we think and/or behave as we do. *Understanding what consti-*

tutes a clean motive is probably the most difficult step in becoming charactered.

Clean motives are the heart and soul of becoming charactered. Without them, one's life experience is ultimately empty and insincere. We discover most about ourselves in the quiet of our own minds. Looking at our motives is often painfully disturbing. However, facing ourselves ultimately enables us to choose our path and forgive others for paths they have chosen which may contradict or violate ours.

"I SOLD MY SOUL!"

Sean was a man whose direction in life took a sudden twist when he married his first wife; a twist that would eventually cost him his soul. Handsome, powerful, popular, and wealthy were the adjectives people most often used to describe Sean. At forty-five years old, he was the envy of his colleagues and his sons.

Twenty-five years earlier, Sean was the class clown in his fraternity at college. One night he placed a lighted cigarette butt in his sleeping roommate's buttocks. This event proved to be only one of numerous pranks Sean pulled off throughout his undergraduate years. A full-blown Yellow, he embraced life and lived it fully in the present. Rounding out his college experience, he served as student body president and enjoyed an athletic scholarship. When the frivolity ran too high, he would quiet himself by hiking alone in the mountains or playing the piano he had mastered as a child.

"I remember exactly when I lost my way," Sean related to me one day. "I was madly in love and wanted to marry this girl in the worst way. Her mother considered me a 'limited partner' at best and quickly dismissed me as a potential son-in-law. She relentlessly criticized my playful nature, asserting that I would 'never amount to anything' in life. Something snapped inside me and I vowed to prove this woman wrong.

"As fate would have it, I did prove her wrong," he continued. "Well, actually I did, and I didn't.

"Against this woman's wishes, I married her daughter and quickly discarded my Yellow nature in favor of a more power-driven Red profile. Subconsciously, I was determined to earn my mother-in-law's respect. Consequently, I lost my wife's. She adored me as a carefree

Yellow and learned to despise me as the jaded Red man I had become. I really didn't do Red well. My primary focus in life became an obsession with proving myself to a woman who couldn't have cared less. It's ironic: I eventually divorced my wife, but to this day remain locked in a life that defies her mother's cruel prediction.

"Only now, in realizing how much I have attained, do I realize how little my financial success matters to the real me. My motive in achieving this vast empire originated twenty-five years ago with my mother-in-law's rejection. I was dirty. Determined to prove her wrong, I have spent a lifetime abandoning my own path to walk one 'worthy' of her. We haven't spoken for years, and yet she has probably had more to do with my life's direction than any other human being."

He signed "I don't even know how to play practical jokes anymore. Board meetings take precedence over hikes or playing the piano. I lost me for a woman who doesn't even care if I exist. I have spent a lifetime with my creative talents and irrepressible energy developing a multi-million-dollar corporation that has little meaning. Everybody is terribly impressed with my life but me. I realize now that I sold my soul.

"And for what? What meaning does it have to abandon the lifestyle I loved when I was young? What value does it have to make money but never have the time to enjoy the simple pleasures money can't buy? I was never happier a day in my life than those crazy college days. I threw me away to prove something to a woman whose daughter I'm not even married to anymore. Now, that *is* bright! And I have only myself to blame. She threw out the bait, and I took it—hook, line, and sinker! Now I understand that proverb, 'If you go to bed with dogs, you're going to wake up with fleas.' No wonder I have been itchin' all these years."

Sean had sold his soul when he allowed his dirty motives to consume his life. Regardless of his colleagues' praise and his sons' envy, he knew he was incomplete and untrue to the path he preferred to walk. He had abandoned himself and worn a mask, disguising his true self from everyone for twenty-five years. The world adores financial success, so none would challenge his self-delusion. Years down the line, he met and married a woman who could see him more clearly. But he had so fully embraced the disguise that any efforts on her part to have him remove his mask were quickly rebuffed until she, too, became part of his lie.

Eventually, Sean had seduced both sons into his prosperous life, sabotaging their efforts to complete their college education by offering more money to join him in the company. Both sons suffer from severe low self-esteem, which can be directly attributed to their abandonment of personally preferred paths in order to embrace a lifestyle "worthy" of their father.

What goes around truly does come around. The same disservice his mother-in-law had offered him he had now forced on his sons. And so the baton is passed from one generation to the next. Each generation is less aware of the cost and more dulled to the eventual price one must pay for dirty motives.

How tragic our motives can be when they damage the very lives of those for whom we live. Unaware, we pass our dirty motives on to those most closely linked to us, even as a mother passes nutrients in her milk to a newborn child. Innocently they are beguiled, entreated to join us for a while along the limited path we have chosen to walk. Subtly, in time, they are stripped of their self-confidence and personal power. Their passion for living which they might have chosen, given clean motives, merely becomes a haunting memory of what they once hoped to become.

It is not too late for Sean to clean his motives and find the charactered path in his life. Anyone willing to clean up their motives can do so, at any time. However, dirty motives will always exact a price. In order to become charactered, we must accept the price and pay our dues for having dirty motives prior to embracing a new path with a clean heart.

"You can't teach an old dog new tricks" simply isn't true with humans. However, the longer one's motives remain "dirty," the longer and more difficult the process of "cleansing" one's motives will be. We become comfortable with the ruts we have chosen. Comfort zones often deny us easy access to our higher selves, enticing us with old, more familiar turf.

Fortunately, becoming clean has relatively little to do with others, and a great deal to do with you. If you choose to become true to yourself and walk the charactered path in life, you must experience humility. With humility comes aloneness. Embracing humility, you must courageously face yourself in the mirrors others hold before you, exposing the painful reality of your limitations. Yet if you are willing to face yourself, you will find within yourself all that is necessary to walk the charactered path. You will find your way to serve others with a clean heart! Ironically, once you have found the charactered path, you will most likely return, eventually, to those who once refused and mocked you, and kindly entreat them to seek the charactered path as well.

Enter patience. After you courageously lift yourself from the dark abyss that your dirty motives have placed you in, you will find that it is only through genuine surrender that you find peace. Despite all you have done to wrestle yourself free of your unclean past, you must humbly rely on patience to clear your slate and grant you access to a renewed future.

How clean is your heart? What treasures do you pursue on your journey through life? What path have you chosen to walk? What kind of traveler through life have you chosen to be—a *victim,* a *villain,* or a *hero?*

Victims would like to make a cocoon in preparation for their transformation to butterfly, but fearing the unknown they stop short and return to their grounded existence. They admire those who walk the charactered path and may even join them for part of the way, but abandon their trek when it becomes too difficult. They spend tremendous energy seeking excuses for their limitations rather than opportunities to serve.

Villains have completely abandoned the charactered path, as well as the healthy path, because of their dirty motives. Their insecurities cause them to spend their lives trapping others as victims in their "caged" existence. They operate out of the motive of fear rather than love, and use the optimum character motive of service as a means to *their* end, rather than as an end in itself.

Heroes embrace the fullness life offers. They are motivated by love, not fear. They share their innate gifts freely and seek to learn the innate gifts of other colors. Heroes stretch to enhance the lives of others, refusing to live for themselves alone. They accept that the winter times in life are inevitable, and learn to appreciate the solace that comes with the spring.

Throughout our lives we select the role of a victim, villain, or hero, depending solely on the nature of our motives. Accurately identifying, understanding, and cleaning up our motives is difficult. Cleaning up motives requires being one hundred percent accountable. Only heroes fully accept responsibility for themselves. Victims and villains always blame others for why their lives don't work.

SUSAN

Susan was a quiet woman: attractive, creative, and determined. This proper lady, bearing a very Blue personality, came to see me after years of marriage to a very Red man. Bill was powerful and his life was filled with ambition. He met his challenges in the business world with the utmost confidence. For years, they reared a family and made their fortune. Yet, they both knew they were living out scripts filled with lies that could only be rewritten through a changed lifestyle. This change would require charactered honesty or senseless divorce. Divorce? How could their success end on such a tragic note? Their friends wouldn't hear of it. Even Susan and Bill struggled with the possibility. Yet they both knew that their motives for maintaining their marriage were not clean. What looked good on the surface was crumbling underneath the weight of their dirty motives.

Susan, Bill, and I worked together for over a year in therapy. Susan blossomed as she learned truths about who she had been and what she could become. She finally learned to like herself enough to admit that she didn't like, or accept, the things she had done in their relationship.

Susan had been both victim and villain in her twenty-five-year marriage to the man she would now divorce. As a Blue, the feeling of obligation to her children had overwhelmed her and "caged" her in a dysfunctional relationship with her husband. Her low self-esteem and self-doubt convinced her that she could never meet the inevitable financial obligations she would face as a single mother. She did what so many unhappy yet frightened victims do. Rather then turn down the part, she accepted a major role in the play that would become her life.

For twenty-five years, her script read:

Be unhappy; pay your dues; care for the children; play the part of obedient wife; hate yourself for selling out; bide your time; ask too little of your husband; ask too much of yourself; use your children to replace what you should have had with him; hate your husband for not meeting your needs; hate yourself for not being strong enough to do what you know is right; BE A VICTIM!

Bill also developed a script for himself. It read:

Lie often; ignore your feelings and those of anyone close to you; pay whatever price the business world demands; hide your insecurities; share nothing—emotional or intellectual—with your wife; resent her sexually; seek others sexually because you deserve instant gratification; hate yourself but deny you are unhappy; ignore your wife; berate your wife; make your wife pay a high price for not doing everything in her power to help you justify your personal deceit and public arrogance; begin your role in life as a victim and MOVE INTO THE ROLE OF A VILLAIN!

The roles were scripted and with rare exceptions, both Bill and Susan played their roles to perfection. Various bit players moved about their stage—children, employees, friends. However, Bill and Susan were clearly the leads. This was their story line and the stage belonged to them. This was their life—their chance to choose the role they would play and the script they would follow. They played off each other so well, even in their sickness, that friends and children often wondered if they hadn't choreographed many scenes throughout their play together. For example, he would come home angry and she would feed him. He would forget to ask her how her day went and she would sulk. The bit players took their cues from the main characters and soon played their roles to perfection as well. The husband would complain to his colleagues that his wife was not interested in the business world and unable to help him in his affairs. Naturally, his colleagues sympathized. Susan would whine to her friends about Bill's late hours at the office and lack of consideration for her feelings. They understood all too well how lonely life could be with the successful, yet villainous men they married and quickly commiserated with her.

One day, after years of blind obedience to her self-destructive script, Susan reversed roles and ignored her pathetic life script. She no longer called her weak female friends. She didn't whine while she fixed dinner every night. She simply filed for divorce. She sought nothing but a new role for herself and an opportunity to rewrite her script. She wished that some of the bit players from her old play would consider trying out for parts in her new play as well. Others were not welcome. There were no roles in her new script for their limited character. Those deleted from her new script were furious. "How dare she?" they demanded. "She will fall flat on her face! She would have been smarter to stay in her limited, albeit financially secure world, and be a proper martyr, than to stir the pot and financially struggle to survive."

All Susan's "friends" agreed, except one. One friend applauded Susan for her courage to change her script. Someday she believed that hers, too, would change for the better. But she needed more time. As with all of us who eventually choose to climb the charactered path, she had some traveling down her own path to do; some smaller steps to take before attempting Susan's heroic feat.

Some of Susan's children understood their mother's motives for rescripting her life and chose to play roles in both of their parents' lives. Others resented their mother for her sudden rewriting of the story line, and punished her by writing themselves out of her script. Some responses Susan expected. Others she didn't. Some people threatened to destroy her and send her groveling back to the script she had known too well and played too long.

Displaying quiet dignity and courage, Susan scripted her new role. It read:

Accept, don't expect; pick your own daisies; exercise; live on less; love more; free your heart and your man to pursue the paths both treasure; listen within; share yourself; take new roads home; cry when it hurts; laugh in the mirror; grant bigger parts to healthy bit players in your life; reflect on your old relationships and risk new ones; contribute your innate gifts; taste your food; forgive your ex-husband; discover new passions; lift another soul; plot a new course; fall down and get up again; pay your bills; remember who you were born to become; create celebrations and traditions; stay warm; like yourself just because you breathe; seek universal truths; focus your commitments; balance your life; serve others; clean up your motives—yes, most of all get your motives clean; BE A HERO!

"A *hero*," she mused. "So unnatural, so uncomfortable—yet so right. It feels so right. But I have no role models. No track record. No money . . ." "NO MONEY!" she yelled out loud. "I have *no* money. I must be crazy to think I can pull this off. Who am I trying to kid?"

"You've been kidding yourself all along!" a voice said. "You're not crazy and you *are* going to pull this off. Just keep rewriting your script, one step at a time. Remember, it's simply a new twist in your path. Take the new step. I believe in you. I've been waiting a long time for us to walk this road together."

"Who is that?" Susan cried, rather bewildered. "Why are you mocking me? What do you want from me anyway?!"

Suddenly Susan was silent. Her tears were quiet. That voice. She knew that voice so well. The voice was hers. "How long have I erased it from my memory?" she reflected. "It is simply my charactered self demanding once again to be allowed to breathe."

It came from the same place that currently housed her negative fears. It was her inner core. This voice was not mocking her at all. It believed in her. She had silenced it for so many years when it would cry out to be heard. It was that forgotten friend she had left stranded so alone and deep within her soul.

The voice had become much stronger over the past months of her self-discovery. She knew this voice. This was a voice she could trust. The role of hero would not come easily. She would have great prices to pay. But the role of victim had not come cheap, she thought. For the first time, Susan realized that she had even played a villainous role at times with her husband, children, and friends, denying them all of the wonderful things this new voice would never allow her to deprive them of again. She had chosen the role of *hero* and would script her new play accordingly.

Life is filled with nuances and truth really is stranger than fiction. Susan's newfound self-respect freed Bill to respect himself as well. Once he realized that their scripts were no longer compatible, he did some serious soul-searching on how he became a victim at the hands of unhealthy parents and insincere friends. Victims with ambition often become villains in time. Typical of unhealthy Reds, he found it difficult to accept critical advice from others. However, when he saw his wife through new eyes, he was motivated to consider the ways of the charactered path. Playing the role of a hero, she could now lift him through her example.

Today, Bill and Susan are very much married, very much together. They have decelerated their life to a slower pace and rekindled their commitment to each other and the charactered path. Both have rescripted their lives. Both have become heroes and bless each other's lives. Their clean motives have stretched to bless the lives of their children and all who are fortunate enough to cross their paths as well.

Each role can be played with tremendous variety as well as differing emphasis. However, the reason (or motive behind why) you choose each role is always the critical factor, and there are only two motives for choosing to be a victim, villain, or hero. Your motive is either clean or dirty. Clean motives come from a personal sense of emotional security, sincerity, and genuine love. Clean motives are always rooted in "win-win" equations. In other words, when your motive is for everyone to win or succeed and gain from the decision or relationship, you have a clean motive.

Dirty motives are always based on fear and are bred from personal insecurity and selfishness. The most common equations for dirty motives are "win-lose" (one wins at the expense of another), "lose-win" (one loses in order for another to win), and "lose-lose" (if one cannot win, he makes sure the other can't win either).

Victims and villains come from dirty motives. Fearing to stretch and embrace positive strengths of other personalities, they allow their dirty motives to sow doubts within the individuals a well as within the relationship. Parties dealing with victims or villains generally struggle with serious trust issues.

Clean motives script the role of the hero. Embracing other's gifts, as well as displaying their own, travelers on the charactered path can be trusted to serve everyone. Scripting clean motives and becoming heroes is undoubtedly the greatest obstacle and truest measure of walking the charactered path.

My patients tell me that checking their motives is the most challenging aspect of therapy. It forces a painful awareness of their personality limitations. As depicted in the play *Man of La Mancha,* the process of cleaning our motives is similar to holding the mirror of who we truly are before ourselves in such a bold fashion that most of us withdraw, desperately clinging to less honest forms of self-appraisal. Rare is the individual, whether or not he or she is in therapy, who humbly faces his/her motives in daily living. Yet this is clearly the most critical step to becoming charactered.

Hartman Character Circle

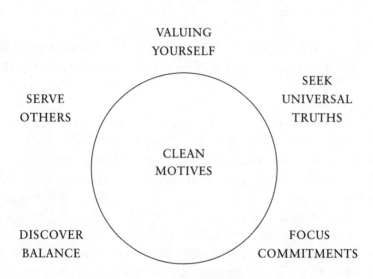

VALUING
YOURSELF

SERVE
OTHERS

SEEK
UNIVERSAL
TRUTHS

CLEAN
MOTIVES

DISCOVER
BALANCE

FOCUS
COMMITMENTS

The central purpose of this book is to enhance our ability to operate from clean motives. Deciphering the difference between a clean and a dirty motive is often difficult, especially when we are not taught it properly as children. Most children don't have adequate role models who can illustrate by their example how to discern a clean motive from a dirty one or as what measures must be taken to live by clean motives.

Reflect on the following scenarios and determine what you would do in each situation. Check my comments at the end of the exercises to determine whether you response represents a clean or dirty motive.

1. Your employer has refused to give you a raise due to a downturn in the economy. You have access to materials from the company that you could sell on the side, generating equal to the amount of money you would have received in your raise. The materials from work would probably not be missed because most of them go to waste anyway. Do you take the materials? Why or why not?

2. Your boyfriend (girlfriend) cheats on you by dating someone else. You have previously agreed to maintain an exclusive relationship. Do you verbally confront him (her) as soon as you discover the betrayal by sharing your evidence and feelings, suppress your feelings (hoping it is just a "one-time" thing), or feel free to date someone of your choosing as payback whenever the opportunity arises? Why?

3. You have applied for a job. During an interview for the position, you realize that a particular question you are asked will put you in a negative light. However, you are equally certain that you are the right person for the position. You see no reason to jeopardize your opportunity by telling the truth so you adroitly sidestep the question altogether. Why or why not?

4. You are separated from your spouse and considering a divorce. You have documents supporting his dishonest reporting of income and decide to present it to the IRS just in case you decide to divorce him. You believe it would give you a stronger position if spousal support becomes an issue.

5. Two couples are unable to produce children and you are pregnant. Abortion and keeping the baby are not options for you. Both couples have approached you about adopting your child. One couple offers you $10,000 while the other couple has very limited funds but you feel is better suited to parent your child. You have an outstanding debt of $10,000 to your parents, which you have never felt capable of repaying until now. Which couple should get your child? Why?

6. You are a manager of a small department within a large company. You have been requested to lay off one employee due to budget constraints. You have been with the company for more than ten years and have become somewhat lazy in your work performance. You have one employee who always makes you look good because he willingly follows through on specific work assignments you have neglected but brings nothing else to the company as a whole. The other employee refuses to cover for you but brings a tremendous energy and strong skills to the company. Which one goes? Why?

7. Your marriage is on the rocks. Your flirtatious wife has accused you of being "out of step" with the times. You enjoy a great sex

life together and have wonderful children. She entices you to drink alcohol, go skinny-dipping with friends, and other assorted behaviors despite how uncomfortable it makes you feel. She applauds your efforts but you continue to feel as if you are betraying yourself and your principles. What should you do? Why?

The "Why," of course, is the critical piece that exposes your true motive for choosing your response. You will always notice that in life, clean promotes clean and dirty promotes dirty. In other words, when you are living life with predominantly dirty motives, it is much easier to select behaviors stemming from dirty motives. However, when you have typically selected clean motives in your life, it is more difficult to choose the "dirty" motive response. *The greatest human triumph comes when an individual changes course from primarily living a dirty-motive lifestyle and selects a charactered, "clean" response.* However, people rarely have any idea how difficult it is to alter your normal responses once they have become a part of your life. People who do not typically lie, for example, cannot begin to appreciate the difficulty involved in being honest for an individual who has chosen to embrace a life of lies.

Selecting a dirty-motive response always leads to a dead end despite its alluring presentation. All the skilled justification or rationalization in the world won't save you from its dark alleys. Seeking the clean-motive response will always prove abundant and enhance the quality of your life as well as the lives of those with whom you interact. It has always intrigued me how difficult it can be choosing the clean motive when, in the end, it always produces better results.

It behooves each of us to examine the accepted motives which drive the groups we belong to. We must explore our personal values to determine whether we are in agreement with our associates. If all the members of your peer group believe lying is acceptable, you must decide whether you agree.

Too often, unaware, we allow our environment to determine our path. The son who resents his father for never being home when he grew up often becomes the workaholic because it is all he knows how to be. The motive may be a number of possibilities: 1) subconsciously trying to please his father; 2) taking the easy path he is most accustomed to and staying in his comfort zone learned as a child; 3) a new perspective that his father's absence was, after all, not an altogether bad thing since he grew up okay; or 4) an honest belief as an adult that being a workaholic is rewarding. Only the charactered individual will make the effort to accurately sort through his or her motives and face the truth.

Throughout life we must ascertain our motives. We are all paupers when we understand the massive limitations we place on our lives by weaving webs of deception regarding our true identities and what we were born to become.

I was never so free as the day I discovered that I was a workaholic. A Yellow workaholic. However, I had always wanted my father's approval. He was a workaholic and if that's what it took to attain his approving nod, I was glad to pay the price. Ironically, this entire script was written unaware in my subconscious. It was only when I brought it to the surface that I could attempt to honestly face my dirty motive and the tremendous price I was paying with my own family. Because I am so playful and fun-loving, the similarity of being a workaholic to my more serious Blue father never occurred to me. I was weaving my web of deception, unaware. Regardless of our awareness, our true motives drive us to walk paths with serious consequences.

Cleaning our motives is the most perplexing, exhausting, yet consequential step of becoming charactered. With it, each step becomes more vital and significant. Without it, each step remains isolated and limited in value. Clean motives provide the foundation for quality living. Without them, all gifts that we develop necessarily remain questionable and inconsistent. Clean motives provide the rich soil that nourish each of the other steps as they grow in adverse conditions of an inclement environment as well as our own limited understanding.

GUESS WHO'S COMING TO DINNER?

One couple refused to examine their motives for years of a tempestuous marriage. The Red wife would scream and yell for any reason, making one up if necessary. She was never content with her White husband's behavior. He would retreat from her anger to their bedroom and simply lock the door. Once she realized that her childish behavior had once again cost her access to her bed, she would race upstairs and beat on the door, begging his forgiveness. Actually, she was probably determined that since she couldn't sleep, he should not be allowed to either.

The irony was that he wasn't even home. He would climb out the bedroom window and sleep with their cook. She bore him two children before he legally terminated the marriage with his wife. For years, his wife would fall asleep on the hallway floor after long, dramatic harangues at her husband, certain he was traumatized on the other side of the locked bedroom door. For years, he slept like a baby after making love to their cook in the servants quarters. Imagine the needless grief both heaped upon themselves and each other simply because they refused to face their dirty motives. The Red wife was so emotionally insecure that she would attack him in an effort to keep the "upper hand." Her dirty motives were to win at his expense (win-lose) and convince him that she was right about everyone's relationships. He responded to her with passive-aggressive behavior, which is always dirty. Rather than confront her directly, he found sexual, emotional solace in the arms of another woman, while his wife slept on the floor outside their bedroom (win-lose). Neither grew up emotionally or learned clean motives, which would have freed them to love or leave each other.

YOU GET WHAT YOU DESERVE

Each time I meet with a patient, I make it clear that I am only prepared to talk about his or her psycho-social-spiritual health. So often, they remark, "But what about my spouse? Do you know that he/she does . . ." Teenagers blame parents and vice versa; employers blame employees and vice versa. If we remain in any relationship for any period of time, we deserve what we get. Some motive, somewhere, keeps you connected.

Honest appraisal and acceptance is the most challenging part of cleaning up our motives. Most patients would like to spend endless hours explaining how they have been hurt by another person, when they should be far more interested in deciphering why they stayed in such an unacceptable relationship, consenting to such perceived abuse. We must face ourselves and be accountable for our motives—whether they are dirty or clean. It is only in understanding the nature of our motives that we can assess their significance in determining the paths we choose.

With rare exceptions, when I see individuals who are ready to leave a long-term relationship, I request that they remain in the relationship for six months while they get "cleaned up"! Before they engage in new relationships, vulnerable to creating the same mistakes twice, I challenge them to discover all *their* limitations that were responsible for their dysfunctional relationship. There is tremendous personal power in cleaning up our motives. Charactered people demand personal power. They refuse to be victimized by life's cruel twists and unexpected turns.

Cleaning our motives is a full-time job. Initially, it seems futile in a world that refuses to reward it. Eventually, and with great personal sacrifice, it simply becomes a way of life. Each individual must personally choose to be clean in motive. Flags will not usually wave, money will not necessarily flow, and people will not always applaud the charactered life. So clean motives must be reward enough.

The question of the charactered life will always be rooted in the simple yet penetrating question, "Why do I think, feel, and behave as I do?" If your motives are unclean, they must be replaced. This is the sole premise on which charactered individuals earn their trust.

WATERFALLS

In our backyard, we enjoy a beautiful waterfall that often reminds me of how life regenerates itself. It provides an inviting ambiance for writing or casual conversation. The filter must be cleaned regularly to maintain its pristine charm. After a severe wind storm one year, the waterfall became clogged and required a plumber.

As our gardener explained the problem, I thought of my work in psychotherapy. People experience "wind storms" that clog their filters and block their life's flow. They literally shut down, unable to free themselves of the debilitating debris. Most people spend years blocked, or at least temporarily clogged, due to painful life experiences.

Once we have learned to clean our filters, we are able to share our insights with others who have experienced life's "wind storms" and been unable to free themselves of the damage. The optimum motive of service keeps our filters clean and teaches others how they can also flow more freely through life by our example. One day I saw a patient I had not seen for more than a year. She had grown dramatically in mastering the six steps of becoming charactered. However, she was quite frustrated with her husband's limited personal development.

"He just seems so trapped in himself," she said. "I know I have wronged him in so many ways for so many years, but I have changed so much and feel so little shared passion with him now."

She was seriously contemplating divorce, something she had never wanted to do because of her own traumatic childhood. I wanted to know more about her dysfunctional childhood and how she had freed herself of its negative control.

She told me of being transferred from a small country school of only ten children to a city school with more than two hundred students.

"I was terrified!" she said. "I was so shy and frightened and didn't dare talk to anyone about it. My teacher, Mrs. Pickney, was ghastly strict and would make us stand up when we gave answers and even walk to the blackboard to show our work in mathematics. One day, in fear, I ran out of the room and hid in the bathroom. She came after me and I locked the door to my stall and stood on the toilet seat so she wouldn't see me. She left and within five minutes I looked down and saw the principal's shoes right in front of my locked door. I was terrified, but to make matters worse, he seemed to know I was there.

" 'It's all right, Rebecca,' he assured me. 'I won't hurt you. No one will hurt you. Come out and have a little chat with me.'

"He came as close as anyone ever came to making me feel loved," she continued. "He loved to dance and so did I, but I never dared ask anyone. He would take me down to our gymnasium and dance with me. I felt so special. I never did tell him what I was afraid of at school. He just seemed to care more about me than whatever it was I refused to tell him.

"Years later, I often fantasized about this wonderfully kind man who saved me from my intense shyness as a child. Whenever things were bad with my parents, or even my husband, I would fantasize that I was with my principal dancing in the gymnasium. I could shut anyone out if they frightened me enough," she said.

"You spent years afraid to face your dysfunctional childhood and now you have overcome it. Yet you are still afraid of your husband, aren't you?" I asked. "You have used this kind, elderly man to save you in your mind's fantasy from this real man with whom you share your life."

She nodded.

Rebecca's motives for a divorce were not clean. She was still motivated by fear. Her "fantasy shield" was sabotaging her. It protected her from facing uncomfortable relationships, and more important, from facing herself. She had one more step to take first. The grace that this kind, elderly man had offered her as a child must be extended to her husband. Rebecca was the vehicle through which the message must be passed.

"I think it's time," she said, "for me to invite my husband to the gymnasium for a dance."

For the first time, her cocoon began to break. The kind, elderly principal had extended himself unselfishly to her, and now she was being asked to extend herself with clean motives to her husband. Who would have guessed that such a request would await her in life? Who would have thought that such a shy child would one day be willing and capable of extending her frightened but firm hand to the man who terrified her as much as the strict schoolteacher had many years before?

Cleaning our motives, like the waterfall filters, frees us, once again, to flow. Humbly identifying that we are clogged is the first step. The second step is courageously facing the question of "why." Once we assess ourselves accurately, we can properly dispose of the debris.

In cleaning our motives, we must listen to others with insights into our behaviors we are blinded from seeing. The Hartman Character Profile will help expose your blind spots. Seek other's opinions and perceptions. Consider the source of your feedback. However, remember that truth comes from many sources. Be humble enough to hear truth regardless of the style in which it is presented, or the source from which it comes.

This step requires daily effort. With practice, it becomes easier to catch your "dirty" motives. Trace your reactions from your initial conscious thoughts to your eventual behavior. Most reactions have an even deeper subconscious rooting which will take time to accurately identify. For the immediate present, stop yourself between your conscious reaction and subsequent behavior. If you are operating on irrational impulses, you can begin to correct yourself rather than continuing to foster dysfunctional behavior.

Find someone to cross-check yourself. Select someone you can trust to be candidly honest with you. Agree to a three-month period when they will strictly play the role of "police officer" to keep you aware of your behaviors. Your current behaviors are so natural that you may be surprised at how many dirty motives drive you without even a second thought. Your police officer will help you sort through your current thoughts and behaviors. Choose someone you can be comfortable with because his or her role is thankless and yet crucial to your success. At least every week, reevaluate your lifestyle and consider what insights you have learned about your daily motivations.

Keep a journal. It helps in reviewing your attitudes and behaviors. You will be surprised at how many daily interactions stem from a single motive.

Be kind to yourself. This process of cleaning your motives requires time and patience. Learn to laugh when you discover dirty motives you have always considered clean. Discuss your insights with others who understand, and seek their advice and support in adopting new ways to think and behave.

This step of cleaning our motives is the binding tie for the entire character-building process; the foundation that gives consistency to our eventual flight. Clean motives build trust in ourselves and invite others to trust and believe in us as well. With clean motives, we role-model the charactered path for those who struggle to understand its life-affirming magic.

CHAPTER SEVEN

Step Four:
Focus Your Commitments

Life is either a daring adventure, or nothing at all.
—HELEN KELLER

Strange, it seems, why so many people spend a lifetime focusing on unrewarding obligations rather than passionate commitments. Can we be so naive about who we are and what we were born to become? To experience life without passionate commitment is to merely survive. To walk the charactered path, to *live* life, requires focused commitments to yourself, to universally true principles, and to serving others.

COMMIT TO YOURSELF

Reds innately understand the importance of committing to themselves. They make plans and set goals like a duck takes to water. I remember the night my Red daughter had an eight-year-old friend over to spend the night. I can still see them, pen and paper in hand, listing all the things they were going to accomplish the next day. True to their core motive of power, Reds recognize that the best defense in life is a great offense. They will not be denied an opportunity to passionately pursue their commitments in life.

The adventurer John Goddard was true to his Red personality, as well, when he committed at a young age to embracing life as a full-blown adventure.

Highly motivated as a youth, John listed a hundred life experiences he wanted to achieve before he died. His list included a variety of events such as navigating the Nile, reading *The Bible*, and hot-air ballooning across Europe. At the time we met, he had accomplished seventy-five of his original hundred experiences and added twenty-five more he hoped to achieve. True of all healthy Reds, Goddard is greatly respected for his focused commitment to himself and the lifestyle, at a young age, he vowed to experience.

> *Throughout the years, there were men and*
> *women who took their first steps down*
> *roads armed with nothing but their own vision.*
> —AYN RAND

DANIEL BOONE

Daniel Boone is best known for his rugged, mountain-man independence. We see him traversing the wild terrain in search of new horizons. But his true life story provides some fascinating insights about keeping our commitments to ourselves both passionate and current. At sixty-five years old, Boone looked across the bedroom at his beloved wife and said, "It's getting rather crowded around here, don't you think, honey? Let's go to St. Louis, Missouri, and make a new home for ourselves where there is room without knocking into everybody." They packed all their belongings and moved to the edge of civilization. For several years, they built a new, rewarding life together. Suddenly, Boone's wife died. He moved far from town and the comforts to which he'd grown accustomed. He left civilization and created a frontier lifestyle.

Daniel Boone valued himself and believed in his commitments. His legendary life is preserved in the American history books to teach us the power of passionately focused commitments.

My second daughter has a White personality. She has struggled her entire life to find her niche, sandwiched between her Red and Yellow sisters. Her sisters would run for student body president and win. She would seek class treasurer and lose. Her sisters got A's and B's without opening a book. She earned D's with the help of a tutor. Like Daniel Boone's early years, Summer appeared destined for a life of mediocrity.

However, like Daniel Boone, she was dissatisfied with her life. Frustrated by her dyslexia and her passive White nature, Summer struggled to hold her own with her successful sisters. For hours, she would cry about feeling powerless to discover her path or find any reason to commit to herself.

I don't know when or how her personal fire of commitment to herself ignited inside. I only felt the warmth of its flame. In seventh grade, when most young people shrink from accountability, Summer took flight. She humbled herself enough to find her gifts. With courage, Summer risked meeting quality people and created meaningful friendships. She excelled in dance and became a freshman cheerleader. She asked her teachers for permission to sit in the front row of each class and to tape their lectures. She often fell asleep while listening to them at night. She eventually earned a higher grade point average than both of her sisters. She did it by successfully focusing her commitments to herself with purpose and passion.

Another White personality too quickly discarded by society, yet triumphant in his personal commitment to himself, was Albert Einstein. He is one of the world's greatest minds and made remarkable contributions to society. However, as a young boy he attended a private elementary school where his father was quickly rebuffed one day when he asked the school headmaster what profession he would recommend young Albert to pursue.

"It doesn't really matter," the headmaster replied. "He'll never make a success of anything."

Focusing our commitments is such a personal experience. It comes from deep within ourselves. Only we know the convictions of our hearts. Only we can commit ourselves to this heroic life filled with inevitable pain and ridicule by those seeking merely to survive life in the role of a victim or villain. Neither genius nor wealth nor good luck can deliver a passionately committed life. The rewards come unexpectedly long after fantasies of fame or fortune have been forgotten. A life of focused commitment requires the persistence of a plow horse. They are not much to look at, but full of substance and capable of enduring to the end.

COMMIT TO UNIVERSALLY TRUE PRINCIPLES

Committing to ourselves is just the beginning in mastering this important step of becoming charactered. The charactered path simultaneously requires a commitment to principles of universal truth. Principled people are empowered and capable of empowering others to passionately live committed lives. Obedience to principles lays the foundation from which we earn other's trust and respect. Principled living provides consistency. We sleep better knowing that the sun will rise in the morning and that a charactered friend will not change his heart and reveal a shared confidence.

I CAN SLEEP WHEN THE WIND BLOWS

A young transient applied for employment on a farm in Kansas one afternoon. There were numerous applicants for only one position as a farmhand, so the farmer asked each young man why he should be hired for the job.

Unlike the other applicants, the young transient replied, "I can sleep when the wind blows."

Three times the farmer asked the question and three times the young lad gave the same reply. The farmer considered it rather odd, but noticed that there was something solid about the young man. The farmer's curiosity about the youth finally got the best of him, and he hired him for the job.

Weeks passed and the new farmhand proved to be a steady asset, although there was nothing particularly impressive or noteworthy to report. One night, without warning, a raging wind caught the local residents by surprise. It was tearing apart loose equipment and leaving its deadly mark everywhere. The farmer tried, in vain, to roust his young farmhand from bed to help him secure his farm.

Irritated by his noncompliance, the farmer quickly abandoned the sleeping youth to set out and desperately secure the place himself. What he encountered would cause him to never again question his decision to hire the lad. Without fanfare, the young man had secured everything on the farm and could comfortably sleep while the wind blew. His life was focused on principled commitments. Paying his dues in advance, he could be trusted. Charactered people accept the price for principled lives and willingly pay their dues.

TIGHTEN YOUR BELTS

Early in my professional career I worked for a nonprofit health organization with a strong public image and hearty fund-raising department. At a crucial time in our expansion, a professional fund-raising corporation recommended that we allow it to handle all future fund-raising activities. It was clearly the easier path to take as charity dollars were becoming more competitive. One group believed we should accept the professional corporation's offer to become our fund-raising arm, while the other felt such a move was certain death. In the end, it was clearly a matter of motive: safety and fear (both dirty motives) versus building our confidence (a clear motive).

Those who chose the professional fund-raising solution *feared* personal responsibility for raising money in lean financial times. I was only a novice to the business world, yet I will always remember the passionate commitment in the speech my boss gave.

"I joined this organization," she began, "because I believed in its message and I believed in the people who were carrying the message to the public. We have offered successful programs for years and continue to be the leading nonprofit organization because of the tremendous need for our services. We have, however, become soft over the years. Our success has weakened our resolve to simply work harder during the lean times. We have become fat and must tighten our belt rather than loosen it another notch. Our eyes must be focused on creative solutions rather than passive acceptance of an easier path. If we go with this professional fund-raising corporation, we will be out of business, and out of the public eye, within the decade. Our only option is to tighten our belts."

A vote was taken and the professional fund-raising corporation was hired to assume full responsibility for all future financial matters. Within the decade, the organization became almost laughable, delivering fewer services with less quality and falling dramatically from the public's view. Our decision to loosen the notch rather than tighten our belts cost us our very existence. We refused to accept the price of principled commitments and pay our dues. Ironically, payment was still made—simply later, more painfully and with less honor.

We don't escape our dues in life, we just postpone the eventual pain. We would do better to tighten our belts up front, pay our dues, and focus our commitment to principles of the charactered path.

Each of us is responsible for discovering and embracing a principled life. Principles such as integrity, loyalty, and perseverance do not come cheap. They challenge us to face our limitations and become accountable in overcoming them. The third dimension of focused commitment is committing to others. In order to serve others, we must earn their trust. To do so, we must sacrifice our innate limitations for strengths expressed by personalities other than our own.

FINDING A CAUSE

Replacing our innate personality limitations with charactered principles challenges us to our very core. To overcome our limitations we must have a cause, something to inspire us when change strikes fear in our very souls. Scholar and historian W. Macneile Dixon once aptly wrote: "If you would make human beings happy, give them a task and a cause, and the harder the better. It is when the gods call them that men rise to the crest of their powers; then they become themselves gods. Their greatness lies in their dreams."

Becoming gods, however, is not an easy task. Remember, Rome was not built in a day. One step at a time, we will discover our way. Lao-Tzu said, "A thousand-mile journey begins with one step."

You may randomly select any biography of any individual who has offered a lasting contribution to humanity. Some were born noble; others knew only poverty. Some were famous; others were known only within their native land. Some were brilliant; others demonstrated significant courage. Yet each of them shared one common trait: Every individual who makes a lasting contribution overcomes debilitating personal limitations through uncommon persistence.

The dictionary defines persistence as "going on resolutely in spite of opposition, to persevere; to remain fixed in character; to be insistent in the repetition of a position, or a question, or an opinion."

To show uncommon persistence requires an uncommon cause. There can be no greater cause than the third dimension of focusing your commitments in the service of others. This blends the powerful fourth step of focused commitments with the optimum motive of becoming charactered, which is service. To serve others, we must be committed to principles of the charactered path. We cannot lift another unless we are on higher ground. We must make a total commitment to achieve success.

The following lists provide the possible limitations each personality must successfully overcome to steer a course toward service and walking the charactered path.

REDS

1. Their obsessive nature blocks their attention to necessary details.
2. Their abrasiveness earns disrespect from potential companions.
3. Their unwillingness to see "people problems" are capable of sabotaging their visionary plans.
4. Their overprotection of an exaggerated ego (insecurity) keeps them from receiving feedback.
5. Their pride.
6. Their unapproachability makes it difficult to bring their plans to fruition.
7. Their self-importance makes it hard to begin at the bottom or do menial tasks.

BLUES

1. Their Perfectionism. ("If it can't be perfect, why do it?")
2. Their low self-esteem diminishes the chance to implement creative ideas.
3. Their focus on personal limitations.
4. Their unrealistic expectations of themselves and others.
5. Their concern with petty issues and others' opinions.
6. Their lack of vision and confidence to act.
7. Their attending to others' lives makes it difficult to focus on their own.

WHITES

1. Their feelings of being overwhelmed in implementing change.
2. Their inability to communicate with others about their fears.
3. Their discomfort with confrontation.
4. Their preference for isolation.
5. Their willingness to compromise their values and beliefs for the sake of peace.
6. Their distress at the effort needed to prove their point (they can be lazy).
7. Their indecisiveness and hesitancy to risk.

YELLOWS

1. Their self-centeredness and and their need to seek instant gratification.
2. Their lack of commitment to the long, difficult path.
3. Their hypersensitivity to others' criticisms.
4. Their concern with looking good superficially rather than making a meaningful contribution.
5. Their scattered thinking and lack of discipline, which irritates others.
6. Their disorganized lifestyle, which lacks focus.
7. Their fickle loyalty breeds contempt.

COMMIT TO SERVING OTHERS

A farmer had a barnyard full of animals who loved him for how well he treated them. One day prior to his birthday, the pig, hen, and cow were discussing various gifts for his birthday. Each felt something special was in order for his birthday but not one knew what to give. They finally agreed to think about it and meet the next morning with their recommendations.

The next morning, the hen and cow arrived already in agreement on the gift they wanted to give the farmer when the pig arrived.

"Good morning, Piggy," they both said. "We have been talking and have decided that Mr. Farmer gets up very early and works hard to make our lives pleasant in the barnyard. On his birthday, he deserves a special breakfast in bed."

"Cow will bring the milk," chortled the hen.

"And Henny will provide two delicious eggs!" mooed the cow.

"And you, Piggy, get to provide the ham!" each snickered with delight.

Piggy, being the introspective type, thought deeply about their proposition, reflecting on the price of his gift versus theirs.

"Perhaps we should give this birthday gift some more thought," he said. "What for you is but a minor inconvenience is for me a total commitment."

Our greatest gifts will always require our total commitment. Our most meaningful contributions can be given only after stretching to embrace the strengths of the other colors. If we are ever to know the beauty of the crags in the highest mountain tops, we must leave our cushioned lifestyles and soar like the eagles.

History is full of men and women who moved beyond minor inconveniences in order to passionately render their lives in the service of others. These remarkable individuals often speak of their committed service as though they were "called" from a higher power to serve. They exude all the gifts necessary for walking the charactered path: humility, courage, and grace.

Florence Nightingale discovered this path early in life. As a young woman, she felt called to aid her English countrymen who were fighting overseas during the Crimean War. Her wealthy father threatened to disown her if she abandoned the comforts of their home. Her fiancé promised to sever their engagement. Many thought her behavior was at best inappropriate; venturing into places a woman ought not to be. Undaunted, this focused woman inspired hundreds of women to join her cause. These committed souls bandaged the wounded, read to the disheartened, wrote letters to the families, and rendered countless services without reward. Many of the women felt ignored, emotionally abused, and tremendously discounted, and left their nursing posts prematurely. They returned home to the comforts of England. Still, many refused to be denied their finest hour of committed service. With Ms. Nightingale at the helm, they remained involved and held thousands of men's hands while they recovered or died deaths with dignity. Today, Florence Nightingale is known as the mother of the noble healing profession called nursing.

There are so many unsung heroes with focused commitments in the service of others. Charactered people serve wherever they can during the various seasons of their lives. Parents who unselfishly give of their time and resources in order for their young children to find their path in life; employers who use their entrepreneurial skills to hire thousands and compensate them with self-respect and financial gain; friends who stretch to speak another's language; children who discipline themselves, freeing parents of constant worry and anxiety; employees who give freely of extra time and talents beyond expectation or compensation. Like Florence Nightingale, these committed souls will not be denied. They feel passionate about the causes they serve. They know what they are about and focus on what it is they must do to accomplish their goal. The hunter who chases two rabbits at the same time will lose them both. These individuals get what they go after. They passionately blend their commitments to themselves, universally true principles, and service to others. We are all the grateful recipients of their committed ways.

Find someone's life to bless. Find something larger to which you can commit. Study it; prepare for it; embrace it. Like the eagle soaring high in the sky, you will never feel more alive than when you are in love with your commitment. Different for you than for me, it will call to you by name and challenge your ability to tame it. Your motives must be clean in order to hear it.

Simultaneously, there must be opposition in all things. When you hear the call to serve, fear will knock on your door, suggesting an easier path. Fear promises to be your constant companion; it will never leave your side.

The charactered path offers no guarantees of comforting companionship. Your solace must come from within yourself. You must remain resolute in the face of ridicule and rejection to bestow your gift on those you came to serve. You must walk some of the way alone. However, as with those committed individuals who have gone before you, you will become less concerned with others' permission to risk, and more enticed by your opportunities to serve. Committed to yourself, universally true principles, and to serving others, you will find your destiny. Your finest moments will come in uncommon hours.

It matters little what your life has been. It matters a great deal what it will become. It has been said, "Whatever you can dream, you can achieve." Focused commitments simply reflect dreams in the making. Go ahead. Make your dreams come true.

> *"Come to the edge," he said.*
> *They said: "We are afraid."*
> *"Come to the edge," he said.*
> *They came.*
> *He pushed them . . .*
> *and, like the eagles, they flew.*

—GUILLAUME APOLLINAIRE

CHAPTER EIGHT

Step Five:
Discover Balance

My favorite study on human behavior was only recently released. A group of researchers asked several thousand individuals one question: "Looking back on your life, what are your regrets?"

The research team wanted to know what these individuals would have done differently, given their hindsight. In retrospect, what about their lives would they have changed?

The only criterion for participating in the study was age. Every participant was over ninety years old. The results of this amazing study helped guide me in my struggle on the charactered path. If we can not learn from the elderly, who can we trust to teach us? There is something about elders that I like and trust; something about their perspective that lends credibility to their responses. Wisdom accepted from another's heart can be less bitter than wisdom earned through personal life experience.

Their responses, as documented by the research team, have served as my model for discovering balance. The answers given by the elders were as varied as the individuals themselves. Some responded with complete details while others summed it up in one word. Compiling the responses, the research team looked specifically for patterns. After months of reviewing their findings, the research team placed the respondent's "regrets" into three distinct categories.

The elders' comments provide a wealth of insights about the balance in our lives. Participants considered their family, friends, employment, religious affiliations, health, and a multitude of lifestyle details. Gathering months of research, the team agreed that the elders' responses could be most accurately expressed in the following three "regrets":

1. *They would have contemplated more throughout their lives.*
2. *They would have risked more throughout their lives.*
3. *They would have left a more meaningful contribution.*

THEY WOULD HAVE CONTEMPLATED MORE

The best-educated human being is the one who understands most about the life in which he is placed.
—HELEN KELLER

From an early age, Helen Keller was both deaf and blind. She displayed remarkable courage in overcoming her handicaps to develop a clearer perspective of who she really was and the life in which she was placed. Reflection brings objectivity and clarity to one's life. Of the colors, Blues and Whites find reflective activities most congruous with their innate personalities.

Looking back, many of the elders discovered they were often in too big a hurry merely surviving the daily madness to reflect on what was really important. Thinking back, they would have made different choices for the use of their time and energy. Men, for example, would have taken more vacations with their families, danced longer with their wives, and spent more time with their friends. Women, on the other hand, wished they had more fully developed their personal interests, laughed more at themselves, and been less concerned with life's petty incidents.

Time to contemplate what we are all about in life helps us to focus on more positive directions and commit to healthier relationships. Often we climb the ladder of success only to discover that the ladder we are climbing is leaning against the wrong building. In our efforts to get to the top, we neglect to look around at where our ladder is leading us.

One Man's Reflective Regrets

Bill raced through life, flaunting his vibrant Red personality, with little time for reflection. He won the corporate wars and successfully launched his children. He never connected with his Blue wife or himself. He lacked balance. His pace eventually caught up with him after his wife left him because he refused to address his alcoholism. Devastated, he finally woke up to his skewed world and joined Alcoholics Anonymous. Working hard to rebuild his life, he shared some candid thoughts.

"Looking back, I see it more clearly now," he began. "How foolish I have been. It seems that I naively followed the path so many men pursue. As young boys, we grow up relatively content to be with friends and family. Somewhere between twenty to twenty-five years old, we strike out to make our fame and fortune. At fifty-five years old we suddenly begin to realize that we've been fooled along the way.

"We realize," he continued, "that money isn't everything. In fact, we come to accept that we really don't need much money at all. We almost revert to our carefree childhoods, to becoming the playful young men we were prior to climbing the ladder. For me, I enjoy time with my children, grandchildren, and friends. I look at my wife, who is such a class act, and wonder how I could have been so blind to her while I was climbing my way to the top in my career.

"I have no regrets for creating a successful business," he said. "I loved competing with the best of them, but I was in overdrive and didn't have a clue about balance. I missed so many moments of really living the life my wife kept inviting me to share. I was too busy scaling new heights to be bothered.

"Every time someone challenged me, I really thought they were just envious of my success," he said. "How arrogant of me! The real kicker is that after our children left home, my wife went back to work. After all, we had very little in common thanks to my myopic obsession with work. Ironically, she achieved more career success in five years than I did in twenty-five years. She just kept it all in perspective."

As a busy professional, I still reflect on my wife and my early years of marriage. Still, I appreciate those simple meals and juggling schedules with only one car. Some days my wife and daughter would ride the bus for more than an hour just to surprise me with lunch. I rode to my first job interview on a bicycle. Our first home was so close to the neighbors that the bored wife would often visit my wife and complete conversations we had begun the night before.

As adults, we must reflect on our lives often. Balance is not something we can create in retrospect. This step requires a daily blending of reflection and risk to make a meaningful contribution to others. Life is made up of moments in the present, not past losses or future goals. If we are not clear about our values and what we are all about, we may discover too late that we missed the mark. I learned this poignant lesson quite unexpectedly one Sunday afternoon.

The Brunch from Hell

All six of us were seated around the table for Sunday brunch—one of our favorite family traditions. For brunch, everyone dresses up and we spend hours talking about a myriad of topics, but mostly about each other. Just being together is what makes it fun. This brunch, however, was not fun. What had always been a cherished memory quickly deteriorated into a nightmare.

We were at a popular restaurant on the ocean and the place was crowded. We began with our typical convivial conversation but quickly lost control. I remember being completely overwhelmed, frustrated, embarrassed, and angry by the end of the first course in our meal. Our children (ages four to twelve at the time) were clearly out of hand, or so it seemed to me. Unable to restore a sense of dignity to our brood, I suggested that everyone just eat and forget any further conversation. It was like somebody had us on candid camera and refused to turn it off. The longer the meal went, the more exasperated I became. To this day, I can't remember exactly what happened, but as soon as we were finished eating, I asked my wife to take our children from the table while I paid the bill.

I sat alone, relieved to know the nightmare was almost over. The embarrassment would soon disappear and the other customers would (I hoped) forget we ever existed. I quickly paid the bill and made my exit.

Two tables from where the nightmare occurred, an elderly man stopped me. He was dining with a younger female companion.

"That's quite a family you've got there, son," he said.

"I'm sorry if we disturbed your meal," I said quickly, apologizing.

"Disturbed?" he asked puzzled. "On the contrary, you have delightfully candid daughters and a most gracious wife. My lady friend and I were just commenting on how fortunate you are to have such beautiful women to enjoy over brunch."

Completely baffled, I could muster nothing more than a blank stare. Surely he was being sarcastic, I thought.

"Tell me, young man," he said, "do you realize how fortunate you are to have children who speak their minds and clearly enjoy spending time with you?"

"Why, yes," I lied. "I suppose I do appreciate their candor and enthusiasm."

Seeing my apprehension, he reached for my arm, and said, "Please don't wait until it's too late to appreciate what you've got!"

This whole encounter was beginning to feel quite odd, and I started to leave, when I suddenly saw him awkwardly remove his glasses to wipe a defiant tear.

Feeling awkward, I looked at his lady friend. Kindly, she took the man's hand. "You must forgive Jim," she said quietly. "His wife left him when his children were very young, about the age your children are now. He was impatient with their irritating mannerisms and childish behavior. That was many years ago, but he has never forgiven himself for what he did to destroy his family. Whenever he sees a family like yours, he realizes how very fortunate you are and wishes he could have just one more chance to appreciate what he once had. He's just hoping to save you from some of the unbearable pain he has faced every time he sees in other children what he never appreciated in his own."

My head was racing with reflections stirred by this couple's remarks. Grateful for their honesty, I thanked them and left. That man will probably never know the gift he gave me that day. I have never looked at my children the same since our "brunch from hell." From the moment when the man's tear exposed his sincere devotion to a family he will never know, I have tried to *never* allow my petty irritations to replace my deep devotion to my children. His wisdom, painfully paid for with years of remorse, has saved me a lifetime of regret. My children and I owe much to this man who touched my life.

One of my greatest literary discoveries on the art of contemplation is *Gifts from the Sea* by Anne Morrow Lindbergh. Rich in wisdom about reflection, she guides her readers through a remarkable journey into themselves. If you want to treat yourself, purchase the book on tape and spend an afternoon in the sun listening to one of the best works I've heard on this vital dimension of being balanced on the path toward becoming charactered.

All that we have in life is choices: how we spend our energy and time and how we will balance our lives. The legacy we leave for those who follow us depends on what choices we make. Unbalanced individuals march like caterpillars who, refusing to reflect, unwittingly fall in line behind the caterpillar in front of them, forming a circle. Like so many men and women who naively follow each other's path, the caterpillars march to each other's pace, encircling the same path until they eventually die from exhaustion. Tremendous energy and significant lives are wasted simply because they don't stop to reflect on where they are going and what they are all about.

THEY WOULD HAVE RISKED MORE

People who risk reaffirm their relationships at work and home with the gift of hope. They see life as an adventure and enjoy opportunities to learn interesting things, go different places, and meet new people. They trust the sun will shine again despite the darkest storm. They affirm that damaged lives will once again recover from their diminished light. They excel where others seek safe refuge from fear of failure. Risk takers embrace passion throughout their lives. Unrelenting, they grasp each moment life offers and invite others to join them in their celebration. Reds and Yellows typically find this element of balance congruous with their innate personalities.

Clearly, the elderly people in the study wished they had risked more. For example, the hot dog stand one man dreamed of opening at twenty-one years old no longer frightened him as it had in his youth. He would have risked opening his stand given the same opportunity again. Another woman remembered the new neighbor she ignored because she felt intimidated. "Today, given the same chance again," she reflected, "I would greet her with a smile and an invitation to dinner."

Looking back, the elders would have embraced life more freely, risking rejection, financial setbacks, and other discomforts often connected with risk. Too late, they had discovered the key to becoming balanced included risk.

Balanced living requires a commitment to taking risks; to doing the things you value. Charactered people know their values and pay whatever price is necessary to experience them. *The stomach shrinks when it's empty. So do the souls of people who stop trying on new hats in life.* We must fill our lives with creative options for which we are willing to put ourselves on the line. Risking keeps us on the cutting edge of life.

A Risking Lifestyle

Consider your lifestyle. Have you chosen a high- or low-risk profile? Do you thrive on change or tradition? Have you embraced a lifestyle of risk or the safer route of caution?

Lifestyle can be seen as the unique patterns in your daily life. It's your out-of-bed-with-a-bounce greeting each morning, or an I-can't-cope-without-a-cup-of-coffee grope. It's the food you eat and the people you avoid. It's both the kind of car you drive—its shape, color, and accessories—and it is the seat belt you regularly use or often ignore. It's saving money systematically or constantly overdrawing your account. Does your lifestyle reflect a healthy balance of positive risk patterns?

Lifestyle can be seen as the daily choices you make. It is your choices about using drugs or alcohol. Lifestyle is getting in shape or giving in to the bulge. It is participating in active sports or cheering from the bleachers. It is pursuing a hobby with a passion or passionately flipping the television channel remote controls. It is getting out or staying home. It is accepting clutter or cleaning it up. Do you make positive risk choices?

Lifestyle can be seen as the attitude you carry in life. It's being positive or negative. It's how you handle stress, conflict, or loneliness. It's knowing how to relax. It is how you feel about your job, your family, and friends. It's being able to change some things in life and coping with the things you can't. It's contentment or despair. It is using safeguards or taking needless risks with your health. It is learning how to deal with emergencies or feeling helpless. Do you have a healthy attitude toward risk?

Lifestyle can be seen as your unique patterns, choices, and attitudes toward risk. Question your current patterns. Are your choices of risk healthy or self-destructive? Do your attitudes reflect a balanced perspective? Risking is a vital dimension to a balanced life. Without risk, reflection has little meaning. Once we identify our passions, our purpose, our path, we must risk whatever is necessary to make them a reality in our lives.

There are, of course, both positive and negative risks. Positive risks spring from the desire to expand one's life with an affirming energy. Positive risks do not limit life or cause unnecessary injury to oneself or to others. Rather, positive risk taking inspires relationships and invites opportunities to experience a more abundant life. Negative risk taking finds its roots in self-absorption and ego-driven needs. It attempts to fill emotional voids in one's life with inappropriate gambles, which often abuse or negate quality of life. Again, we need look no further than the reason for engaging in the risk-taking behavior to know whether it is positive or negative.

Marriage is risk. Children are risks. Employment is risk. Losing weight is risk. Facing ourselves is risk. For that matter, getting up in the morning is risk. But to not risk is to die. Alfred, Lord Tennyson once wrote: "To strive, to seek, to find, but not to yield." To walk the charactered path, we must press forward. We must make healthy risk choices, develop positive risk attitudes, and establish productive risk patterns.

Judy always enriched our group therapy sessions with her optimism and positive energy. She traveled over two hours each way for our sessions without complaint. On her way home one week, she missed her exit (she was singing with the radio), and found herself twenty miles down the road before realizing it.

Undaunted, she decided to exit at the first opportunity and explore this new community she had never seen before. She found herself in the middle of a barrio and she spoke no Spanish. She discovered a mall and stopped to shop. She later said that she had felt like she had won a free trip to Mexico.

She enjoyed herself because she trusted herself and embraced the adventure. There was no need to panic or whine; no need for anger or blame. Magical to watch, she was optimistic to the last mile, making an escapade out of most people's worst nightmare.

People who risk pick and choose their life battles carefully, refusing to waste energy on the inevitable mishaps and curveballs that life tosses. They act rather than react. They refuse to be controlled by the petty concerns that consume frightened people's lives.

Personalize your life. What is pure magic for one person may have limited appeal for another. Charactered individuals find room for a multitude of risks in their lives. They tolerate vast differences in the preferences of those they encounter in life. For them, rigidity is the enemy. The charactered path simply cannot be walked without risk.

THEY WOULD HAVE MADE
A MORE MEANINGFUL CONTRIBUTION

The three most significant days in your life are:

1. The day you were born.
2. The day you find out why you were born.
3. The day you discover how to contribute the gift you were born to give.

Perhaps our greatest contribution in life is the one we give of ourselves to those we leave behind.

Many of the elders participating in the research study acknowledged that one of their significant regrets was not contributing more quality time to those who would miss them most with their passing. The ultimate motive of the charactered soul is service. How can we serve those we love when we don't even recognize who they are?

A bright, articulate couple was successfully climbing life's ladder, the envy of all who knew them. Bill was a medical doctor with a tremendous thirst for life: He loved boating, was a genius with computers, and relished competitive sports. Lynda was an avid reader and a tennis enthusiast as well as a loyal friend. Her priorities, however, were clearly defined by her role as mother: She was devoted to their two small children.

Bill wanted to please her, but because of his many interests, he always fell short. He wondered if he could ever satisfy Lynda's emotional needs. During one particularly hostile argument, Bill held Lynda's arms, looked right in her eyes, and said in desperation, "What is it you want from me anyway?"

Quietly, without hesitation, she answered: "Right now I would accept walking to our mailbox together to get the mail." She understood her priorities, while he struggled to juggle his relationships, career, and interests.

The less time and energy we spend on those we love, the less capable we are of loving them. If you've aligned your priorities with those determined by your peers to be acceptable and correct, don't look to the world for help if you find them lacking. In general, people are so impressed with your "success" that they are incapable of providing useful insights regarding a charactered life.

Years later, when Bill and Lynda temporarily separated, he realized his mistake. He hadn't understood what Lynda meant by "just being together, even if it meant walking to the mailbox." When they separated, he entered a world of painful reflection and hurt. One night, several lonely months into the separation, he penned this letter and poem to her:

My dear Lynda,

Since you left, I have had some time to think. I have many regrets; the biggest one being how I missed you when we were together. In piecing together the puzzle of what happened, I wrote this poem for you, entitled:

MISSED MOMENTS

Now I have the time . . .
. . . to share my feelings
. . . to walk on the beach
. . . to see your softball game.

Now I have the time . . .
. . . to open your car door
. . . to walk to the mailbox
. . . to take you on a picnic in the park.

Now I have the time . . .
. . . to hear your endless chatter about nothing important to me,
but everything important to you
. . . to lie quietly by your side and watch you breathe
. . . to laugh at mutual jokes.

Now I have the time . . .
. . . to fall in love
. . . to learn why you love the rain
. . . to take that college class together.
Now I have the time . . .
. . . where are you?

Postscript: This couple did commit to each other again and fell in love. They struggled at first to find and maintain the balance between family and career but have successfully met the challenge. He remains forever grateful that Lynda valued herself enough to demand a balanced perspective. She remains forever grateful that he was humble enough to accept a balanced life.

Nature teaches the importance of balance. I remember camping as a young boy and being taught that the laws of nature must be respected. Charactered individuals do not defy natural laws, be they laws of nature or laws of psycho-social-spiritual health. They simply learn to obey.

Consider the essential balance the four seasons offer. To eliminate any of the seasons would create inevitable collapse in the world's ecosystems. Yet we often neglect the balance and swing to extremes. For example, the watchword for the 1990s is "eliminate"; it's time to dump surplus. We search for ways to clear away the clutter of our lives, as more of us adopt tenets from the simplicity movement. We no longer want it all. Having it all was exhausting. We simply ran out of time, energy, and money.

Balance frees us from the "stuff" that keeps us from enjoying what

we really love to do. Perhaps the Shakers had it right when they sung a favorite hymn, entitled, " 'Tis a Gift to Be Simple, 'Tis a Gift to Be Free."

To live simply and wisely, we must know our values and make those values central to our lives. Goals are good, but we must not be prisoners of them either. We also need to set time aside to rest. Recent studies clearly indicate that getting away from a particular task gives us renewed clarity and productivity when we return to complete the task.

Balance requires sacrificing part of our natural selfishness for an overall commitment to serve. When we balance ourselves at the center of our lives, we develop a personal power which allows us to help others become centered. "Centering" requires sincere reflection and positive risk taking.

Control the Center

Winning basketball teams must control the ground around the basket, called the "key." Controlling the key, they are able to dictate the action. Regardless of how proficient a basketball team may be at shooting from outside, they will not win without controlling the "center" under the basketball hoop.

Unbalanced individuals live their lives on the fringes of the "court." They are not centered. Balanced people know and control their center core values. Such a man was Bill Hall. Bill was a teacher working with a group of hardened street juveniles in a New York City junior high school in East Harlem.

Bill used the game of chess to teach them the necessity of "mastering the center" in order to win at sports, and more important, at life. He initiated a rivalry among his students, whom he called his Royal Knights. He established round-robin competitions in which each team member played others. He challenged the students to create new strategies that could be useful in tournament play. "Learn from your opponent," he told them, "but always control the center of the chessboard."

Bill presented the game of chess as an exciting adventure. He always asked his students what they learned from each opponent.

While he always paid attention to the game's basics, he also taught them the power in stretching to master new strategies. By respecting the basics of the game and motivating his players to blend new thinking with the old, Bill created a dynamic winning team.

His young students lived unbalanced lives on the fringe of society. Poor English skills, limited financial resources, and racial scars dictated their self-destructive lifestyles. Teaching them the game of chess and the art of balancing their lives by centering themselves, Bill transformed their lives and introduced them to the charactered path. With a centered perspective, they were able to express a balanced blend of their innate personality and newly acquired character.

It is said that at our birth God whispers to our hearts what gifts we are to give. We then spend the rest of our lives trying to "remember" what He said, and what we came here to do. Whatever contribution you are here to make will require sincere reflection and considerable risk.

Charactered people look beyond their fears to discover what they love. *We love those we serve, and we serve those we love.* Do not be deceived by the immediacy of merely surviving life. Such limited vision diminishes our ability to know what is best for us in the grander scheme of things. You have gifts. Humbly seek them and courageously bestow them on those you were meant to help find their way.

A healthy man is the complement of the seasons,
and in Winter, Summer is in his heart.
—HENRY DAVID THOREAU

Discovering balance is a personal journey. It requires the perseverance of the Reds, the compassion of the Blues, the clarity of the Whites, and the optimism of the Yellows. Balance cannot exist without a humble acceptance of our innate strengths and limitations, the courage to discover new gifts, and patience to enlighten us as to how, when, and on whom we were meant to bestow our contribution.

Let's think again about the three major regrets:

1. They would have contemplated more throughout their lives.
2. They would have risked more throughout their lives.
3. They would have left a more meaningful contribution.

Reflect for a moment on your life. What do you miss most right now? Where would you like to put more energy? What personal commitments are you ignoring that deserve your attention? There are constant whisperings in our hearts that are often ignored until they pass or get louder. We can respond to these important messages only when we allow them to be pondered sincerely in our hearts and legitimately addressed in our minds. What you pay attention to has a much greater chance of being expressed.

Our greatest regrets will always be the risks we never took. The greatest regret of my college days is that I never took a backpack trip though Europe. Even though I've traveled all around the world, I have never forgotten the lost opportunity of being a young, carefree wayfarer. It is far better to have taken a risk and been disappointed than to wonder forever what might have been. What risk do you need to be taking today?

Too soon our lives are over and most of us wonder where the time went. Consider your childhood, education, hobbies, careers, friendships, travel, family relationships, and the many possibilities your life once held. Where did you feel your greatest connections? Who will miss you most at your passing? Where will your legacy be most fondly remembered? Making a meaningful contribution requires a commitment from the heart. It cannot be a charade. There can be no pretense. *In the end, wherever your heart spent its most sincere energy will claim your greatest contribution.*

CHAPTER NINE

Step Six:
Serve Others

If I am not for myself, who will be for me?
Yet if I am for myself alone, what am I?
—HILLEL

Service is the optimum motive that drives the charactered life. Without the opportunity to give to our fellow human beings, we would remain limited and empty. Mastering each of the five preceding steps is essential to serving others. In fact, the very process of becoming charactered signifies that we can be trusted to serve.

Each step of self-mastery plays an important role in becoming trustworthy. We cannot love others until we genuinely value ourselves. Obedience to the natural laws of universal truth is essential to rendering quality service. Clean motives actually compel us to seek others to serve. We must be focused in our commitments in order to prioritize how we can each best render our service. Discovering balance helps us maintain perspective in our service. Each step is a stretch beyond our innate personalities to more charactered lives. Finally, the optimum motive for walking the charactered path requires that we stretch in three dimensions: spiritually, socially, and psychologically. From the words of William Shakespeare, "Some are born great, some achieve greatness."

SPIRITUAL STRETCHING

Spiritual well-being includes virtues such as love and compassion as well as noble principles such as truth and integrity. Service without spirituality lacks warmth and depth. A sense of humanity and universal truths emanates from this dimension of service. People with spiritual depth don't ask if there is something they can do to help in difficult times; they simply act on their intuition. Unwilling to accept the easy route, they find time and energy beyond merely meeting their obligations.

On a spiritual level, service invites people to resolve their differences at the next *highest* common denominator. Without a sense of spirituality, we respond at the lowest possible (and least demanding) common denominator of agreement between two parties. Spiritual stretching necessarily requires a denial of self, a sacrificing of one's individual preferences for the well-being of another.

Before he converted to Christianity, Sadhu Singh was a Tibetan Buddhist monk. While traveling with a Buddhist monk he had known years before his conversion to Christianity, he experienced an event that would change his life and, ultimately, the life of his disciples.

One winter day at dusk, the two old friends were traveling on foot through the mountains to a remote monastery. In the bitter cold, the monk cautioned Sadhu that any delays could prove deadly and insisted that they arrive at their destination before nightfall.

Suddenly, they heard a cry for help from a man who had fallen from the narrow path to a ledge some distance below. The monk assured Sadhu (and himself) that this was God's way of saying that the man's time had come to meet his maker. Sadhu disagreed.

Replying from his heart, Sadhu said, "This is God's way of asking whether I am willing to serve others in preparation to someday meet *my* maker."

"Sadhu, what value are you to your God, or anyone else, when you are dead?" the monk asked. "Come now, we must hurry for it will be dark soon."

"You go ahead, my friend," Sadhu urged the monk. "To leave this man after hearing his plea would be to die myself."

The monk trudged off alone as the snow began to fall more heavily.

Sadhu traversed down the mountain to find the weary traveler with a broken leg, unable to climb off the ledge. Sadhu immediately knew that the man would die if he left him to go for help. Sadhu made a sarong from his blanket and began the painful ascent up the mountain, packing the weary traveler on his back. After what seemed like an eternity, they were again on their way. Unable to accommodate more weight, he abandoned all supplies on the ledge. They had to reach the monastery to survive. Their path, however, became increasingly difficult to follow, hidden by the freshly fallen snow.

Time passed, and Sadhu suddenly saw an image in the far distance of the monastery, its lights shining through the falling snow like a beacon of hope. With renewed hope, he pressed on. Sadhu was emotionally and physically exhausted, but he refused to quit because of his duty to the man he carried on his back. He simply continued down the path, putting one foot in front of the other and making his way one step at a time. Snow continued its deadly dance while the dark engulfed them. With only a slight moon to light their way, he pressed on, refusing to give way to thoughts of hypothermia, leg cramps, and hunger.

Without warning, he suddenly stumbled and lost his balance. Both men hit a stonelike object in their path. Brushing aside the freshly fallen snow, Sadhu Singh discovered the body of his former traveling companion and friend. The Buddhist monk had frozen to death. Apparently, without reason to go on, the lone monk had lost his will, and tragically, his way.

Years later, Sadhu Singh was asked by his disciples, "What is life's greatest burden?" Without a moment's hesitation, Sadhu replied, "To have *no* burden is the greatest burden in life."

Charactered individuals carry heavy burdens with their compassionate hearts. They stretch beyond themselves in the service of others. Service is the blending of genuine spirituality and psychological truth. Those who would serve must have clean motives and a willing heart to go the extra mile.

SUSAN

"All my life I worked hard to maintain an image of myself that protected the essential me. I convinced myself of who I should be, not who I was. When I started reading *The Color Code,* I understood that it would help identify who a person really is, but I was afraid that I might not like what I would learn.

"I did learn things I didn't like. For a while, I was trapped in the pain of discovering who I really was—whatever 'comfort zone' I had was fading away. I wasn't comfortable with who I was, but changing me was painful. The greatest fear I've felt has been that I wouldn't change. Because I was more afraid of not changing than anything else, I would force myself to do things that were very unnatural and painful for me.

"Self-reliance has been in my thoughts ever since I embarked on this path. I've wondered about some of the bad attitudes it encourages, especially pride: Pride to stand alone, to be unwilling to ask for or accept help from another person, even a person who loves you and wants to help. It limits the depth of love the two of you are able to experience. Before being introduced to *The Color Code,* I would recognize problems I was creating for myself and would attempt to change, but I never got far. I usually decided after a couple of weeks that it wasn't as important as it had been, or that it was impossible to do. Because I insisted on trying to change alone, I missed the encouragement and advice from others, and the knowledge that someone else was pulling for me. Trying to change on your own is setting yourself up to fail. Why would you want to change alone?

"There are three things that I'm learning now that are becoming more a part of me every day:

"1. You can't change without developing patience, especially patience with yourself. No one changes anything without patience. It is not just trying something over and over until it works. It also does *not* include beating yourself up for the times it doesn't work. You have to allow yourself the time it takes to grow.

"2. Being loving and forgiving are the two most important character traits, whether you're talking about others or yourself. Once you're ready to work on them honestly, you are ready to grow.

"3. Submission. Surrender to what is true about yourself, about life, and about relationships. Submission is the one thing that will make everything else happen. It is the only true act of freedom I know. It melts pride, changes attitudes, and allows you to see truth. That sweet feeling of submission is something I can't get enough of. I chase after opportunities to experience it."

Service invites clean motives. We prioritize the important aspects of living rather than becoming obsessed by our own selfish desires. We gain this new perspective through the ultimate motive of service and living the charactered life.

This perspective invites us to deny ourselves our petty personal concerns for the betterment of others. The charactered life is not built on notable sacrifices, but rather small kindnesses and daily triumphs over our inherent limitations. To notice the sun shining in another's eyes while eating lunch and to offer to change places, is to serve. To overcome a personal limitation in order to increase another's trust is to serve. To serve is to stretch.

Perhaps the spiritual dimension of service is best defined by Gelett Burgess in her fascinating book *The Bromide and Other Theories*. I have condensed this brilliant work to a few paragraphs to whet your appetites. The author simply asks:

"HAVE YOU AN EDUCATED HEART?"

Last October I sent Crystable a book. She acknowledged it, and promptly. But two months afterward she actually wrote me another letter, telling me what she thought of that book; and she proved, moreover, that she had read it. Now, I ask you, isn't that a strange and beautiful experience in this careless world? Crystable had an educated heart. To such as possess the educated heart thanks are something like mortgages, to be paid in installments.

Everything can be done beautifully by the educated heart, from the lacing of a shoe so that it won't come loose to passing the salt before it is asked for. Consider the usual birthday gift or Christmas present. By universal practice it is carefully wrapped in a pretty paper and tied with ribbon. That package is symbolic of what all friendly acts should be—kindness performed with style. Then what is style in giving? Ah, the educated heart makes it a business to know what his friend really wants. I have one friend to whom I can't express a taste that isn't treasured up against need. I said once that I loved watercress, and lightly wished that I might have it for every meal. Never a meal had I at his table since, without finding watercress bought especially for me.

Do you think it's easy, this business of giving? Verily, giving is as much an art as portrait painting or the making of glass flowers. And imagination can surely be brought to bear. Are you sailing for Brazil? It isn't the basket of fine fruits that brings the tears to your eyes, nor the flowers with trailing yards of red ribbon—all that's mere kindness, ordinary everyday kindness. It's that little purse full of Brazilian currency, bills, and small change all ready for you when you first trip ashore at Rio.

Is it sufficient simply to offer your seat in a streetcar to a woman? The merely kind person does that. But he does it rather sheepishly. Isn't your graciousness more cultured if you give it up with a bow, with a smile of willingness? Besides the quarter you give the beggar, can't you give a few cents' worth of yourself too? The behavior of the educated heart becomes automatic: You set it in the direction of true kindness and courtesy and after a while it will function without deliberate thought. Such thoughtfulness, such consideration, is not merely decorative. It is the very essence and evidence of sincerity. Without it all so-called kindness is merely titular and perfunctory.

You call once or twice at the hospital. Do you ever call again? Not unless you have the educated heart. Yet the patient is still perhaps quite ill. Once there was one who used to bring a scrapbook every morning, pasted in with funny items about the day's news.

Truly nothing is so rare as the educated heart. And if you wonder why, just show a Kodak group picture—a banquet or a class photograph. What does every one of us look at first, talk about? Ourself. And that's the reason why most hearts are so unlearned in kindness.

If you want to enlarge that mystic organ whence flows true human kindness, you must cultivate your imagination. You must learn to put yourself in another's place, think his thoughts. The educated heart, remember, does kindness [service] *with style.*

SOCIAL STRETCHING

Necessarily, each dimension affects the others. Effective interpersonal relationships require a healthy blend of spiritual and social stretching.

Our lives are shaped by those we love,
by those we refuse to love.

JERRIE

My sister-in-law, Jerrie, *always* has time to serve. Racing at our hectic pace in Southern California, I had learned to ignore threatening sideshows of human violence so often witnessed in my daily life. One such sideshow erupted between a quarreling couple right after we picked up Jerrie from the airport and exited the freeway on our way home.

"Taylor, would you mind pulling over and waiting for a moment while I talk to that couple?" my White sister-in-law asked. "As a former police officer, I feel compelled to see if I can help."

Before I could stop completely, Jerrie bolted from the car and ran back toward the quarreling couple. (She's a professional trained to resolve disputes.) Several minutes passed and I finally joined her to see if I could be of any help. When I reached them, my sister-in-law had separated the couple and requested that I take the woman to my car while she calmed the man down. Eventually, we offered the woman a ride to a safe place until they could both calm down and talk. Days later, still deeply affected by this selfless act of service, I considered how removed I had become from humanity's daily discomforts and suffering.

Some weeks later, our family was beginning a vacation on a back road when we stopped to assist a woman with a flat tire. Rejoining my family after a brief thirty-minute delay, one of my daughters noted, "We shouldn't have stopped, Dad. We could have been a lot closer to our hotel by now!" Not only had I removed myself from humanity, but I had removed my daughter as well.

JESSIE

Shortly after the minister had completed his benediction and the first shovel of earth had been tossed on the casket which lay in its final resting place, the many friends and relatives who had followed in the procession from the church hugged Jessie, whispered sincere condolences, and left. Numerous employees who knew Steve for most of his twenty-five years in the company had taken an extended lunchtime in order to be at his funeral. They weren't able to be at the intimate graveside service because they had obligations at work.

Steve's children were most supportive of their mother through the entire burial process. They had been at her side since their father's tragic car accident but needed to return to their busy lives now that the funeral was over. Steve's best friend had helped with the many funeral arrangements and provided valuable moral support to this woman who had understood and encouraged their close friendship over the years. He offered to wait at the car for Jessie if she felt she needed a few more minutes with Steve at his grave. She thanked him and he walked toward his car.

Here, at last, Jessie found herself alone with the man she had loved for thirty-two years. Her mind kept remembering the life they had shared as a couple. Her tears no longer seemed to carry the appropriate sense of sorrow that she had been taught belonged at funerals. Now her tears were empty, bitter queries of a relationship she had never experienced with a man she had deeply loved.

"Why? Why now, am I finally alone with you?" she asked. "How many nights did I ask you for a walk on the beach, or try to cuddle close in bed, only to be reminded that other priorities came first? You expected me to understand your business concerns and accept your pressing civic obligations. At times when I felt so alone, I would challenge you, but you always had the answers. And if you were desperate for an answer, then I knew I could count on you to tell me how difficult it was for you to express your feelings. I often wondered, Steve, if you ever used that excuse on your boss. Somehow I don't think so.

"And you always had time for our children as well," she noted. "I loved you for that, Steve, and so did they. They will always have fond memories of their dad—the scout master, mechanic, storyteller, and companion. I envy them, Steve, I envy them all, from your best friend to your colleagues at work, and most of all, our children. They had something with you I haven't known for years—a relationship.

"And I want to know why," she demanded. "Did I become unattractive? Did I nag too much? Was I boring or inattentive? Did I have too many needs, or too few? Did you ever really love me at all?"

She began to reminisce, and smiled. "Funny," she said quietly, "it seems ironic that you spent so many hours and so much energy at your work and yet your colleagues could stay only for the funeral.

Even the kids could be interrupted only for a couple of days before they were pulled back into their own busy lives. And here I am, Steve, alone with you still. Perhaps I'm just not finished hoping for a relationship that always could have been but never was."

Now her tears were again the sincere, loving remorse for the loss of her husband, the only man she had ever truly loved.

"I'm sorry, babe, for being less than what I could have been for you. I do love you, Steve. You have always been my Sir Lancelot, my reason for dreaming, my companion. If only we could have experienced in reality all the special moments, caresses, and feelings I continually fantasized us to share, enjoy, and be."

We need to get involved in others' lives in real ways. One of the reasons soldiers share such camaraderie is that they genuinely need each other and they play a crucial role in each other's survival. We are not meant to go through life alone. We are meant to connect and serve each other. Too often we merely pass by each other, whether it be at the office, at home, or on the street. We simply refuse to be vulnerable and make the legitimate connection with the people in our lives. However, when we do make this connection, our lives experiences their highest and most legitimate value.

Serving others frees us from our limited selves. It gives us many opportunities to express our unique gifts and demonstrate why we belong to each other. Much like Sadhu Singh and the wounded man on the mountain ledge, or Jessie and Steve, we are all traveling companions. We deserve each other's joys and heartaches. Serving others requires us to accept others' happiness, as well as their sorrows.

SHARING HAPPINESS

To serve others socially means to share each other's happiness. Others' happiness is difficult to share when we suffer from petty jealousies and bitterness. Uncharactered people always resent others' success, feeling it should be they rather than others who are happy. They resent others' success in life because they are dissatisfied with their own "limited" lives.

These "limited" lives are role-modeled by people like: 1) The couple who ask, "Why do our neighbors have new cars while we still drive this junker?"; 2) The teenager who questions, "How come my friend gets to come home whenever she wants, and I'm stuck with this ridiculous curfew?"; 3) The parent who queries, "Why do the Joneses' children always behave so much better than mine?", and 4) The employee who resentfully wants to know, "Why doesn't my boss promote me when I've been here the longest?" Such questions flow from the selfish individual who is incapable of serving others.

"Poor me," they say. It's the pity party of life. They invite only those individuals who also feel cheated by life and resentful of others' success; people who wouldn't miss a chance to commiserate with them. Notice how they don't extend an invitation to charactered individuals who might "crash" their party. Selfish people do not serve humanity with unconditional love. They are too busy feeling abused or explaining their "hard luck." Like Sadhu Singh's friend the Buddhist monk, they are insensitive to the needs of others. They consider their own burdens (albeit often self-inflicted) to be heavy enough, without incurring another's problems on their journey through life.

SHARING SORROW

Serving others socially means sharing sorrows. Sorrow is especially difficult to share when we are self-absorbed. *Selfishness breeds a life of its own, filled with superficial relationships.* Examples of these limited individuals include the parent who only comments on a child's report card when he or she excels, the spouse who only wants to hear what is going right at the office, or the child who only wants to be told when he's doing something right. Many limited people can't even accept death as a natural step in our shared life journey.

I remember one dying man who was beloved by the entire community. Many friends and family gathered during the week prior to his death to share some parting thoughts with this man they revered and deeply respected. He was in tremendous pain but he delighted in speaking with and touching, one last time, those people he had loved throughout his life. All four of his children adored their father. Only three came to thank him for his many kindnesses and wish him well on his continued journey.

His son couldn't bring himself to see his father in his wretched condition. Furthermore, the son refused to have any part in his father's viewing or funeral. He didn't care how uncomfortable his absence might be for his grieving mother. He felt no responsibility to assist his mother in negotiating the tedious but necessary funeral arrangements. He was still a selfish child at the chronological age of twenty-eight.

Ironically, yet expectedly, this same boy-man was as uncomfortable holding a small child in his arms as he was holding his dying father. He denied his wife the opportunity of having children because of his own selfish desires. Much later in life, his selfish tragedy continued as he and his wife abandoned their dreams for a family, settling into separate vacations and individual pleasures. Frightened and self-absorbed, he never learned to give of himself and understand the meaningful contributions his father experienced through years of sharing both happiness and sorrow in the service of others.

Quite different from this selfish young man was a professor of mine who shared her personal sorrow to save my life. Many years have passed since I was a student in her college class. And yet I can see her still: eyes that penetrate the soul and a heart that always spells a warm welcome. She challenged her students to stretch! One day she showed me how willing she was to stretch as well.

On a beautiful warm spring day, I showed up at my Interpersonal Group Communication Skills class, barefoot and sporting rather long, unkempt hair. She told me I was out of line and expected a conversation after class.

"Taylor," she began after the class was dismissed, "I hope you won't mind me sharing a very private piece of my life with you."

Rather taken back by this vulnerable gesture, I assured her I didn't mind.

She proceeded to tell me about her days as a college coed. She shared how her fears of men and dating kept her cloistered in the psychology research labs running rat studies and exceling in her studies at the expense of her social life.

"I wore large overcoats and men's watches," she remembered out loud, "so I would never invite male attention. They frightened me so much that I simply pretended that I was *only* in college for my studies; that my social life was irrelevant."

"Today," she continued, "I live alone with my dog, my garden, and my academic career. I wasted so much energy hiding from the very thing that I crave—intimacy! If only I had those years back again, I know it would be difficult for me to feel comfortable with men, but knowing the lonely price I have paid without intimacy, I would certainly try some things differently, given another chance."

I sat silently in awe while this kind Blue professor quietly and candidly revealed herself.

Seeing my awkwardness, she proceeded. "I don't wish regrets for you in your life, Taylor. You have been blessed with tremendous people skills and psychological insight. Don't waste your energy, as I did, fighting petty issues of dress standards and mediocrity. You are so much better than that."

I don't recall much dialogue after that. What I remember is how I felt as she shared her sorrow in an honest attempt to free me from mine. She was right about my rebellion. I was as angry at petty collegiate dress standards as she had been at men. As she revealed her pain without attack or guilt, she spared me a lifetime of wasted energy and limited contribution. And her gift of social service didn't stop there (again, the educated heart). Many years later when I first presented *The Color Code* she was in attendance. I was stunned to see her.

"There is no other place I would rather be tonight than right here with you!" she shared with a wink when she saw my shocked expression.

She clearly had learned to share. Genuine service means connecting socially. It means sharing both our joys and our sorrows with those we meet in life.

Sharing ourselves and others' burdens requires genuine risk. Novelist Louise Erdrich wrote, "I hope that the way one appears to others is shaped by all of the edges you have come to in your life and, most of all, by the other faces you have looked into with love."

"I SURE DID LOVE THOSE BOYS"

A young man had completed his doctoral course work in psychology and lacked only his doctoral dissertation. In seeking a topic to study, this young student was informed of an undocumented story about one hundred and twenty-five men currently ranging from ages thirty to forty years old who had grown up in the Bronx, New York. None of the men had experienced any physical violence, legal hassles, or been in trouble with the police when they were teenagers, which was unheard of for boys growing up in the Bronx.

Fascinated by the research possibilities, the doctoral candidate pursued the details of this unusual story. He sought verification from the police that it was not merely a rumor or myth and they confirmed the accuracy of the account for the dates in question. In researching their records, the police, too, were baffled by the lack of disciplinary problems during this particular time in their precinct.

The doctoral candidate considered the possibilities that might have created this scenario. His first task was to find the variable that made the difference in these boys' lives during that ten-year span. He conferred with religious leaders, parents, coaches, community leaders, school administrators, and local businessmen. He checked everywhere, but discovered nothing in the form of a specific variable that would explain the exemplary behavior of these boys over a ten-year span. They represented different races and religions. They came from different families—some single parent, some dual, some divorced.

He asked the boys, who were now grown men—all successful, highly educated members of their communities. They all remembered different sources of influence in their lives from coaches to parents, from religious to civic leaders. Many had touched their lives for good. However, only one individual received their unanimous vote. Each man remembered, almost reverently, one middle-aged teacher who had inspired both their hearts and their minds.

The doctoral candidate was terribly anxious the day he climbed the rickety stairs to this old woman's apartment. She appeared at the door and he wondered if this could be the teacher that they all remembered so fondly. She had aged considerably and could scarcely stand without her walker. She welcomed him into her home. Quickly her eyes began to dance as she recalled numerous personal events from each of "her boys" ' lives. Her eyes betrayed her deep devotion to these young people she had taught in junior high school so many years ago. Hours raced by as she reminisced the "good old days" with each young man's name. She spoke of them as though they were her own flesh and blood and asked about each one. She relished stories about their current successes and cried when sharing details of their personal disappointments.

"Tell me," she asked, "did Robert ever get that baseball glove he dreamed of? Did Romeo marry? What is his wife like?"

Question after question, child after child, he updated her on each of the now-grown men's lives. Before the evening ended, this remarkable teacher had taught him about a variable for modifying human behavior that none of his college professors had discussed. She had taught him about the variable of love. He rose to say good-bye but she asked for one last glance at his photographs of the boys.

Walking him to the door, she paused. She took him by the hand and gently requested, "If you see any of my boys, will you tell them how much I love them and think of them?"

The doctoral candidate was mesmerized. In all his training, he had never encountered something quite as powerful as the love exuding from this wise, elderly schoolteacher. He knew, however, that love would not be clinically recognized as a variable for changing human lives. He could not prove a hypothesis with such data. And yet, for this brief moment as he descended the old rickety stairs, he didn't care. Somehow his doctoral dissertation didn't seem so important. He had experienced a human masterpiece—a charactered soul in the form of a little white-haired teacher whose eyes still sparkled. Her life and her love had touched him, and he could never be the same again.

Charactered individuals not only choose to dance, but also find others with whom they can share the dance. Healthy individuals dance only the numbers they know. Unhealthy people wait for someone else to extend a hand, and sick individuals complain that the music is too loud. With or without the music, charactered souls find reasons to dance and ways to invite others to join them throughout their life!

True character is best displayed in the arena of social relationships. When we offend people with our limited attitudes and/or thoughtless behavior, we are engaging in today's single most grievous form of abuse. When we lift others by sharing our innate strengths and learned gifts, we are engaging in the highest form of life. We must remember that one light is sufficient to bring warmth and guidance to thousands.

The following charts illustrate specific ways that we can serve each other. Each personality color has unique needs as well as gifts. Consider ways your innate personality can best serve and be served by others.

REDS

REDS NEED BLUES:

- To teach them compassion
- To soften their communication
- To point out details
- To promote them
- To encourage their risk taking
- To plan the action
- To confront them directly
- To not take comments personally
- To approve of their style and direction
- To trust them

REDS NEED WHITES:

- To calm them in crisis
- To listen to them
- To bounce ideas off of
- To feel safe with
- To promote compromise
- To delegate responsibility to
- To support them
- To balance them with perspective
- To remind them about quality versus quantity
- To communicate logically with

REDS NEED YELLOWS:

- To teach them charisma
- To converse logically with them
- To accept their leadership
- To cheer for them
- To broaden their myopic vision
- To socialize them and idolize them
- To not take their criticism personally
- To be less scattered and inconsistent
- To teach them spontaneity and laughter

BLUES

BLUES NEED REDS:

- To teach them honest feedback
- To teach them assertiveness
- To get the job done
- To give them specific direction
- To foster a sense of security
- To execute the plan
- To understand them
- To appreciate them
- To include them in plans
- To be trustworthy

BLUES NEED WHITES:

- To show them the good in others
- To teach relaxed attitudes
- To listen to them
- To respect them
- To appreciate them
- To calm their nerves
- To minimize their imperfections
- To carry out specific assignments
- To be agreeable
- To be emotionally responsible

BLUES NEED YELLOWS:

- To keep a healthy "here and now" perspective
- To promote creative, playful moments
- To foster optimism and hope
- To cherish and appreciate them
- To remind them of their intrinsic value
- To make them laugh
- To keep conversations flowing
- To facilitate social relationships
- To promote simplicity
- To share intimate moments with
- To show them the lighter side of life

WHITES

WHITES NEED REDS:

- To motivate them
- To inspire and encourage them
- To lead them
- To share risks with
- To organize them
- To promote them
- To establish healthy boundaries
- To provide vision
- To stay task-oriented
- To set goals and objectives

WHITES NEED BLUES:

- To motivate them
- To be kind to them
- To not make them feel guilty
- To teach them creativity
- To encourage and believe in them
- To direct them
- To build self-confidence
- To nurture them
- To initiate activities
- To accept them as they are

WHITES NEED YELLOWS:

- To excite them
- To encourage them
- To accept their low profile
- To be kind to them
- To slow down
- To be intimate with them
- To keep confidences
- To promote activities
- To share a peaceful relationship
- To be sensitive of their self-doubt

YELLOWS

YELLOWS NEED REDS:

- To focus them
- To praise them
- To notice them
- To risk with them
- To give them freedom
- To allow for their spontaneity
- To keep them on task
- To accept their boundless energy
- To be positive and say, "I'm sorry"

YELLOWS NEED BLUES:

- To give grounding and direction
- To teach compassion and sensitivity
- To notice details and specifics
- To provide stability
- To encourage the completion of tasks
- To remember important events and facts
- To laugh at them
- To praise and notice them
- To provide moral leadership

YELLOWS NEED WHITES:

- To calm them
- To listen to them
- To praise them
- To play with them
- To help them to speed up
- To be tolerant of them
- To share confidences
- To enjoy their childlike innocence
- To share a peaceful relationship
- To accept their crazy spontaneity

PSYCHOLOGICAL STRETCHING

To the corkscrew, the knife is crooked.
—from a letter I sent to my wife

Just as the corkscrew sees the knife through its limited eyes (and therefore the knife appears to be crooked), each personality speaks a different language. This requires us to psychologically stretch in order to understand them. Symbolically, Reds speak Japanese while Blues prefer dialects of English. Yellows articulate best in Spanish while Whites prefer to sign. *You cannot serve other people unless you speak their language or they are charactered enough to speak yours.* Uncharacered people spend a lifetime blaming others for a breakdown in communication rather than taking ownership for their failure to stretch. The problem may be simply recognizing that being in dysfunctional relationships is like traveling in a foreign country with the limited capability of only speaking your native tongue.

Just as the various colors speak in different tongues, so do nations, places of employment, and families. For example, generally speaking, the language of the business world is Red. (Look out for yourself; get to the point; be productive; analyze the data; take risks; and make a profit are credos that exemplify the business world's credo.) Family life is typified by Blues. (Establish traditions; a place for everything and everything in its place; moral integrity; compassion for sickness and social dilemmas; and sit for two hours in the hot sun to watch your daughter tap dance as she passes by for five seconds in a parade, express the creed for quality families.) High technology and international diplomacy are best reflected by Whites. (Be tolerant in understanding another's point of view; kindness costs you nothing; patience is a virtue; silence is golden; and all things come to he who waits are axioms that best explain high technology and international diplomacy.) The language of youth is most inviting to Yellows. (Seize the moment; live for today; live and let live; believe in yourself; and trust in your dreams most accurately reflect the attitudes and behaviors of childhood.)

Recognize how the four personality types affect your life. Become charactered by speaking their language fluently and you will become a welcome guest in the lives of each color. Psycho-social-spiritual health requires that we understand, validate, and successfully communicate with each color. Uncharactered people remain limited in their interactions by refusing to serve others in their language. They prefer to remain with their "colleagues in color," limited by their myopic thinking rather than venturing out to explore the insights and perceptions offered through a myriad of other admirable personalities.

Each personality color becomes a victim when it limits itself to its innate language. Reds often limit themselves through arrogance and selfishness. Their methods include bullying, fast-talking (debate style), and denial of any personal wrongdoing. Blues are limited by their self-righteousness and unrealistic expectations. Their preferred methods include unnecessary guilt, whining, and perpetual discontent. White limitations often come from silent aloofness and intellectualism. Common White methods are hiding out and smiling in agreement but doing whatever they want. Yellows limit themselves with superficiality and avoidance. They generally refuse serious discussions, focused commitments, and deep emotional expression.

Reds bring the gift of vision. They build the bridges in life, but rarely take the time to cross them. They content themselves with thinking that building the bridge is sufficient unto itself, while cheating themselves of the greater value which comes in sharing with others the rewards of their vision.

Blues bring the gift of compassion. They remember others in the special celebrations of life. They go to great efforts to make events perfect, seeing details others would never consider. However, many Blues give their gifts with strings attached, expecting the recipients to demonstrate the same style and sincerity with gifts in return. Sometimes their strings become so burdensome ("If you like the shirt, why don't you ever wear it?") that people reject both gift and giver.

Whites bring the gift of clarity. They genuinely listen without reproach, offering patience and tolerance of another's attitudes and behaviors. However, with their fear of conflict, they often keep their insights to themselves, denying others their valuable perceptions.

Yellows bring the gift of enthusiasm. They embrace the world with their magnetism, lively conversation, and playful interaction. Their candid comments often reveal very little of who they truly are, as Yellows often disguise their inner feelings in fear of painful emotional rejection. A lifetime of masks may cause Yellows to lose their carefree way and eventually shrink from any meaningful social connections.

Stretching to speak another's language frees us from our own self-imposed limitations. Yellows learn to express themselves emotionally when they learn to speak and understand the language of Blues. Whites discover the power of human interaction when they develop the Red gifts of assertion and "bridge building." And so on.

Again, we see the magic of the three gifts: humility, courage, and patience. Humility allows us to see the value in the language of others. Courage enables us to stretch and embrace their gifts. Yet, with all our stretching, we discover that it is ultimately a gift of patience that allows us to learn to speak or understand the languages of others at all. In the end, patience provides a loving hand to lift us the final distance we must climb. *There is no more poignant life experience than to love another so genuinely that we successfully enter their world and invite them to come out of themselves and discover a passion for living.* As Dag Hammarskjöld, former secretary general of the United Nations once said, "It is more noble to give yourself to one person completely than to diligently labor for the masses."

Charactered individuals will always be best remembered for the gifts they stretch to embrace and give from outside the innate color of their birth. Perhaps it is in the stretching to obtain these gifts that we learn to more deeply prize them. This should not suggest that our innate core gifts are not to be highly valued or nurtured. Our natural strengths always assist us in serving others and communicating who we are. Simply stated, the charactered life demands that we give more than our innate gifts. It is the combination of innate and learned gifts that creates the synergy for clean, rewarding service.

To genuinely serve others is to learn the gift of the Blue heart. Rich in self-sacrifice and compassion, they entice us to emulate their commitment to humanity. They hear what others aren't saying; what, perhaps, they may never be capable of saying.

There are countless ways we can serve others. More important than how, is *why* we serve. Ultimately, our motive for service makes the difference in the quality of our lives. We serve for one of two reasons: 1) because we fear; or 2) because we love. Every thought and action we experience comes from a primary motive of either fear or love. Since the results of our service may appear, in the end, to be the same, many of us struggle to decipher the difference in their origin.

The difference in service rendered from love and service rendered from fear is the difference in a charactered and uncharactered life. Though not readily detected in the early stages, lives filled with service from the dirty motive of fear become obligatory and demanding. Those who serve others from the clean motive of love will develop relationships based on honest acceptance and free agency. In order to continually love others from a clean core, we must accept and love ourselves. Loving others requires tremendous energy and self-sacrifice. It cannot be done when our motives are selfish and obligatory. It cannot be accomplished when we pursue limited rather than universal truths. It does not come to those who frighten easily. However, not to embrace service as the powerful final step in becoming charactered is to have not embraced life at all.

The charactered path is steep and covers a lifetime of struggles. It can not be walked when we carry unnecessary baggage (spiritual disguise, social mistrust, or psychological insecurity). To fly like the butterfly, we must free ourselves to love and be loved.

Humility represents the water which must be kept pure if we are to successfully make our trek. Courage is represented by each step we master in order to be trusted to serve. Patience is our acceptance of others to share our path when it becomes too steep or, perhaps, too lonely along the way.

On this vast landscape, all creatures reside within themselves.
Yet, none need walk alone.

—Nina Kremens

COLOR CODE COMMUNICATIONS, INC.

1999 PRODUCT ORDER FORM

515 S. 700 E., Ste. 2E • Salt Lake City, UT 84102 • (800) 761-0001
ilovecolor@aol.com • www.thecolorcode.com

The Color Code
hardcover $22.00   paperback $12.00
The most accurate work on personalities and relationships available. Inspires and motivates quality lifestyling. Vital to understanding personal development and successful interpersonal relationships.

Dealing Effectively with Different Personalities
Six Tape Cassettes $75.00   Our #1 item
Powerful six-tape cassette program complete with excellent recommendations for understanding and successfully relating to each individual color. Numerous examples are provided to assist you in immediate application. Each tape focuses on one of the Four Color Personalities, plus entertaining live presentation overview of Color Coding concepts and the six steps to becoming a genuinely charactered individual. Includes a Personality and Character Profile.

Seeing Red, Feeling Blue, Turning Yellow, and Running Up the White Flag:
Parenting and The Color Code
Single Cassette $10.00
Based on his popular Color Code Personality Profile, Dr. Hartman outlines six things parents can do to ensure children grow to their full potential. He skillfully explains how children think and feel, and tells what it is they need from their parents.

Decoding the Colors of Marriage
Single Cassette $10.00
You will love this enthusiastic presentation on how to make every marriage more successful. Dr. Hartman will inspire you to embrace the six steps that you can take to enhance your relationship with or without your spouse's involvement.

Hartman Personality Profile (Adult or Youth Profile available)
Self-Scoring Profile: Adult $9.95, Youth $5.00
This easy-to-administer and self-scoring Personality Profile has already become the standard for accurately measuring an individual's personality. Profile includes questions, scoring, methodology, honest overview of personalities, and explanation of Profile results. (Please specify Adult or Youth Profile and quantity.)

Hartman Character Profile (Adult only)
Testing Profile $9.95
This powerful testing instrument accompanies the Hartman Personality Profile. Insightful with its clarity on what strengths and limitations an individual has developed from other personalities, as well as their own. Profile includes questions, scoring, methodology, honest overview of character development, and explanation of Profile results.

Satisfaction Guaranteed: Quality performance of our services and products is vital to us at Color Code Communications Inc. We believe in you and want to earn your trust as we develop a mutually beneficial relationship. If at any time, for whatever reason, you feel the quality of our services or products has been compromised, we will make full restitution and guarantee your complete satisfaction.

Other Services: Color Code Communications also provides customized in-house training lectures, workshop, and management consulting. *Please call or write for further information.*

Telephone Orders: 1-800-761-0001. Please have Visa or MasterCard number, expiration date, name, mailing address, and daytime telephone number ready. *Merchandise is mailed within three working days.*

E-mail: ILoveColor@aol.com

Mail Orders: Make checks payable to Color Code Communications. Send order form with check to: Color Code Communications Inc., 515 S. 700 E., Suite 2E, Salt Lake City, UT 84102

Fax: (801) 531-1826

Quantity	Description	Price	Amount
	PLEASE INCLUDE SHIPPING CHARGES. UTAH RESIDENTS MUST PAY 6.1% TAX ORDERS CAN BE FAXED TO (801) 531-1826	(Up to $30) $7.00 Up to $60) $10.00 (Over $60) $15.00	SHIPPING _____ TAX _____ TOTAL _____

NAME: _____ PHONE _____

ADDRESS: _____

CITY _____ STATE _____ ZIP _____

VISA/MASTERCARD _____ EXP. DATE _____